Reflections

OF GOD'S FAITHFULNESS

Finding hope for life's journey

MARLA BRENNEMAN

An **Olive**PRESS**Book**™
from
Olive **Press**
צהר זית
Messianic & Christian Publisher
Rochester, NY 14609 and
Port Leyden, NY 13433

Reflections of God's Faithfulness
Finding Hope For Life's Journey

Published by

Olive Press צהר זית
Messianic and Christian Publisher
P.O. Box 5 6 7
Port Leyden, NY 13433
www.olivepresspublisher.org

Our prayer at Olive Press is that we may help make the Word of Adonai fully known, ... and spread rapidly and be glorified everywhere. May our books help open people's eyes so they will turn from darkness to Light and from the power of the adversary to God and ... trust in ישוע Yeshua (Jesus).
(From II Thess. 3:1; Col. 1:25; Acts 26:18,15 NRSV and CJB, the *Complete Jewish Bible*)

This book has earned the distinction of being called an **OlivePRESSBook**™ because it embodies the concept of being "crushed" to produce the "light" that guides readers to His Light

Cover design by Harriet Miller
Interior by Cheryl Zehr, Olive Press

Printed in the USA
ISBN 978-0-9790873-3-2
1. Spiritual Growth 2. Devotional 3. Inspirational

This book is dedicated to my Lord and Savior, Jesus Christ.
Without Him, I wouldn't be who I am today.

PREFACE

Our church hadn't had a monthly newsletter for many years, so I decided to start one. When I began working on the first edition, a church member told me I needed to write a monthly column. He said it could be called, "View from Where I Sit." My first thought was that no one would want to read what I wrote. But with this person's kind coaxing, I added my column.

I determined ahead of time that the column should be encouraging to others and be real. Each month, I asked the Lord what I should write, and most entries seemed to flow out of me very naturally. Three years later, I began working in the church office and continued creating the newsletter. Through the years people have commented about my writing, telling me how what I shared really blessed them. Some were people I met in other states who had been reading the newsletters on our church website.

What I have gone through has helped me minister the hope of Jesus to others who are going through life's struggles. Because of what He has done for me, I have been able to show them that God is faithful, that He can be trusted, and that He will never leave us or forsake us.

My purpose in compiling these writings into a book is to encourage you. My prayer is that you will be drawn closer to Jesus, our Lord and Savior, as you read about my life. God can surely be trusted with your pain and struggles. I encourage you to take everything that you are struggling with, lay it at His feet, and watch Him work miracles for you. An added bonus is a wonderful relationship with Him, the best friend you will ever have.

I have kept the columns in their original format: one per month. I added a few new entries along the way. The columns can be read as daily devotionals or from cover to cover, as you choose.

I want to introduce you to my family. I have been married to my wonderful husband, Bob, for over 28 years. He works in construction. We have four children. Amber, our oldest, is married to a terrific guy, Matt. She is in graduate school getting her master's in counseling. Matt is working in sales. Kyle, our firstborn son, attends college majoring in economics and philosophy. Jezra, our second son, currently works as a hotel clerk, saving money to continue his schooling in psychology. Breanna is our "baby," although she is over 18. She is in an honors college studying biology. When I wrote most of these entries, our children were in elementary and middle school and we had not even met Matt. Now they are all grown up. I am thankful for the help each of them and Bob gave me in getting this book to press. They all contributed one way or another. I have a wonderful family. I am very blessed!

I would love to hear from you! You can contact me at

marlafb2000@gmail.com

or write to me through the publishing house.

Marla Brenneman

Acknowledgements

I want to thank my wonderful family, who has been very supportive through this process, and the friends who have walked with me through thick and thin. Without all of you, things would have been much worse for me! A special thank you to Barb, Denise, Elaine, Laura, and Rachel, who serve as intercessors for this book.

TABLE OF CONTENTS

Reflections
OF OUR AWESOME GOD

GOD IS FAITHFUL

Faithful. This is the word that comes to my mind when I think back over the last year. God has been faithful to me throughout the year even when things weren't going the way I thought they should. He is faithful as my provider. Whenever we were at a point of not knowing how we were going to make it, God has always come through in providing money to do what we needed to do or in providing a way to do without the money. He is faithful in the way He leads and guides me. Even when I am not sure about the way He is leading me, He is always there helping me see that His way is best. He is faithful in the way He comforts me when things are going wrong or when sad things happen. He always understands my grief and gently helps me accept what happened and move on with Him. He is faithful in the way He disciplines me, not in a harsh, condemning way, but in a gentle, loving way. He is faithful in His love for me, never faltering in that love even when I am unlovable.

My experiences with God's faithfulness can be applied to the body as well. God has been very faithful to us as a congregation, even when we thought things should have been done differently, He is still faithful in showing us what He wants us to learn through these experiences.

Thank you, Jesus, for your faithfulness in 1996. We look forward to seeing more of your faithfulness in the New Year ahead.

GOD'S WINNOWING FORK

JANUARY 1997 (CONT.)   BY BOB BRENNEMAN (MY HUSBAND ☺)

John the Baptist said, "*I baptize you with water for repentance. But after me will come one who is more powerful than I, whose sandals I am not fit to carry. He will baptize you with the Holy Spirit and with fire. His winnowing fork is in his hand, and He will clear his threshing floor, gathering his wheat into the barn and burning up the chaff with unquenchable fire*" (Matthew 3:11-12).

I myself have seen and felt the Lord's winnowing fork run through my life this past year. I have seen this fork applied to others and to those in our congregation as well. It has been a painful year. The Lord is peeling off layers of chaff. This chaff is bondage that keeps us from the Lord and from loving others. The more layers the Lord strips off, the more we can see the seed within. This seed isn't of our works, but the work of the Holy Spirit within.

Will we allow the Lord to continue to peel away the chaff so that His seed will be revealed within us? I am sure that in 1997, "*according to the plan of Him who works out everything in conformity with the purpose of His will*" (Ephesians 1:11), God will bring forth a great harvest as we continue to submit to Him.

GOD'S CONTAGIOUS LOVE
FEBRUARY 1997

This month is traditionally a time to reflect on the love between a man and a woman, but I want to reflect on God's love for us and the love of His people toward each other. We have seen this love in abundance during the illness of my sister. Our local congregation was very good to us in providing a way for Bob and me to go and help my sister's family while she was in the hospital. Numerous people here prayed with us and called to express their concern. My sister's church family came together. They scheduled meals, but people who weren't even on the schedule would stop by with a frozen casserole or other food items. One family brought a bag of sandwich meat and buns for submarine sandwiches, with chips and pop to go with it. People would call and ask if they could pick up anything for us at the store and would not let us pay for it. Others brought cereal and prepared foods to stick in their new microwave my father provided for them. We were overwhelmed with love for these people and so impressed with their generosity. We have witnessed the body of Christ in action in a crisis. Jesus said, *"By this all men will know that you are my disciples if you have love for one another."* (John 13:35) We certainly know that these people are Jesus' disciples! Jesus' love in action is a beautiful sight to see.

This made me think of people like my neighbors who have no church home. They have no one to rally around them during a crisis. What better way to show Christ's love than to organize meals from our small group to these neighbors. Jesus' love is meant to be shared. I will always be grateful to God for letting me see His love in action in such a tangible way!

STEPS TO A RIGHT RELATIONSHIP WITH GOD

MARCH 1997

Peter took Him aside and began to rebuke Him. "Never, Lord!" Peter said. "This shall never happen to you!" Jesus turned and said to Peter, *"Get behind me, satan! You are a stumbling block to me; you do not have in mind the things of God, but the things of men."* Then Jesus said to his disciples, *"If anyone would come after me, he must deny himself and take up his cross and follow Me"* (Matthew 16:22-24).

I have been thinking about the cross and Jesus' death. It was a very humiliating death. I can't even imagine the pain and suffering our Lord went through for each of us. He went through this to have a love-relationship with us as his bride. In order to have this relationship, there are three steps we must take.

The first step is to deny ourselves. I have a hard time giving up the way I think things should happen. I have it all figured out in my mind. I am often like Peter, only looking at things through the eyes of flesh and not seeing them the way God sees them. God's way is always the best way, but usually not the easy way!

The second step is taking up our cross. The cross symbolizes total commitment even unto death. Are we willing to commit to Jesus even unto death? Our cross includes living within our circumstances. A leader in our church said, "Our circumstances are God's harness." Often I want to escape from the harness that is put on me. In Elizabeth Elliot's devotional book, *A Lamp for my Feet,* she says, "When personal relationships break down, it is a sure sign that there is a rift in one's relationship with God."

The third step is to follow Jesus. After we have denied ourselves and picked up our cross, we are ready to follow Jesus. He doesn't usually give us an "itinerary" to follow with all the details spelled out in advance. He just shows us the first step which can look very hazardous or scary. When we take that step, then He shows us the next one. It is a lesson in trust every step of the way.

The reward comes as we step out into what He is calling us to do. It brings fulfillment. It builds our faith. We get to know the Lord better. We become sure of the One we are trusting.

As we approach Easter, we can celebrate the death and resurrection of Jesus because we know that wherever He leads us, He has been there before. Thus we know He understands our pain and struggles, and will never leave us or forsake us!

JURY DUTY!
APRIL 1997

I was called to the jury on Monday, March 10th. Thursday of the same week, I was supposed to go with Jezra on a field trip to an aquarium. It was required that each second grader had an adult with them for individual attention. Jezra and I had looked forward to going for over a month. When it was my turn to be interviewed by the lawyers, one of them asked if there was any reason I couldn't serve on this jury. I told him about the field trip.

We took a break right after my answer. All the other prospective jurors were saying they were sure the lawyers would excuse me. "He sounded very sympathetic to you," one said.

When we got back in, they named the people in the jury box who were excused. My name wasn't among them. I was to serve on the jury! I was very unhappy, sure that I would have to miss the school trip. There was some hope in my mind that it could end on Wednesday, but not much.

On Wednesday at lunch recess, the prosecution hadn't rested yet. I was sure there was absolutely no way I would get to go with my son. I figured if the defense had half as much as the prosecution, it would take at least another day to get to deliberation. When we got back from lunch, the prosecutor stood up and said, "The prosecution rests, your Honor."

The defender rose and said, "The defense rests, your Honor," without ever presenting anything.

Hope sprang up in me then for the first time.. Before I knew it both lawyers were giving their closing arguments. We were deliberating by 3:20 p.m. After the verdict, the judge and the attorneys came in to let us ask questions we had about the case. As I was leaving after the question time, I told the judge I was so glad to be able to go on the trip with my son.

"We knew you would," he replied, as if I should have known, too.

The judge could see the whole picture. He knew the evidence the lawyers were presenting. He knew there was only a slight possibility that the trial would last past Wednesday. I was the one all bent out of shape with worry the whole week because I was so afraid I would miss that special memory-building time with my child.

God, like the judge, sees the big picture. We must trust Him. We often get too worried about things in our lives. God sees it all. We can trust Him to bring it to pass. All the worrying in the world will not change the facts. We must trust God even with our deepest desires. He knows what we need and He always has our best interest at heart. We can spend our energy trusting Him, or wear ourselves out with worry. I want to trust Him!

Trust in the LORD with all your heart and lean not on your own understanding; in all your ways acknowledge Him, and He will make your paths straight (Proverbs 3:5-6).

FATHER'S DAY

JUNE 1997

As I think of my earthly father, I think of all the things he has taught me. An appreciation of God's creation, an excitement for the Bible as he made scripture come alive with his commentaries, and a heart for reaching out in love to others without thinking of getting something in return. Think about what your father instilled in you and the importance of an earthly father. God is mostly referred to as a father, so fathers must be very important. To know the love of a father is the greatest joy on earth. But even if you did not have that kind of love from your earthly father, God is offering you a perfect father-love. God the Father really loves us! *But because of His **great love** for us, God, who is rich in mercy, made us alive with Christ even when we were dead in transgressions--it is by grace you have been saved* (Ephesians 2:4-5). I am just recently learning what this kind of love is all about. God loves us no matter what we do. There is nothing we can do to stop this love. We were loved long before our earthly parents brought us into this world. Wow! I pray that we all may *"grasp how wide and long and high and deep is the love of Christ, and know this love that surpasses knowledge--that you may be filled to the measure of all the fullness of God"* (Ephesians 3:18-19).

God's River Of Revival
July 1997

I had a "vision" from the Lord the other night as I crawled in bed. I "saw" a huge, flooding river overflowing the banks, uprooting trees, houses, and other things in its path. It was as if I was in the river and could hardly stay above water, scared to death that the debris would hit me. I asked the Lord, "Who or what is safe during this flood?" It looked as if everything in its path was being destroyed.

At that moment, I could see right through the muddy rushing water to a fish that was swimming in it. I could tell the fish was totally enjoying the rushing water. It was like a playground to a child. This fish was at home in the water. It didn't matter how furious the water was; this fish could survive and even enjoy it.

The Lord spoke to my heart, "*My daughter, the people who will survive my river of revival will be the people who already dwell in my presence, who know how to breathe in the presence of the Lord. When the rushing river of revival comes, these people will be able to enjoy the water and not be drowned by it.*"

I want to dwell in God's presence. I want to be in tune with His spirit and swim in the presence and power of God. I pray that we will all be able to survive the rushing river of revival when it comes.

My eyes will be on the faithful in the land, that they may dwell with me; he whose walk is blameless will minister to Me. No one who practices deceit will dwell in my house; no one who speaks falsely will stand in My presence (Psalms 101:6-7).

BECOMING LIKE A CHILD
AUGUST 1997

And He said: "I tell you the truth, unless you change and become like little children, you will never enter the kingdom of heaven" (Matthew 18:3).

The other evening I was watching as an 8-month-old baby would take off crawling across the floor toward his destination determined to get there. Whenever my kids tried to stop him, he would just crawl around them. The only way to stop him was to pick him up. Are we that focused on God's plan for our lives that we are determined to get there no matter what obstacles are in our way?

Have you ever watched a child explore the outdoors for the first time? As soon as they are old enough to observe the world around them, they notice everything. If we look at the world through their eyes, we will see it in a new way. Everything is there for the child's exploration. We should have that "exploration mentality" with the new things the Lord is doing; an anticipation of what the Lord has in store for us.

Children are also so trusting. They take you at your word. They believe that you will do what you say. They believe whatever you tell them. We need to have that kind of trust in God. As adults, we start to reason things away. We have a hard time taking God at His word. We need the faith of a child to make it in our walk with the Lord. Jesus, help us to "change and be like little children." Help us have the kind of faith that takes You at Your word, explores the new things You are doing, and determines to get where You are calling us no matter what the devil throws our way.

FACING OUR GOLIATH

OCTOBER 1997

Greater are You who lives in me than any Goliath I must fight.
Greater than all my enemies, using what they mean for harm
for good in my life (from the song, *"Greater Are You,"* by Mark Altrogge).

There are times in my life when I face the "Goliaths" of depression and anxiety. These giants look so huge and immovable when I look at them with my human eyes. They're big, I'm small. They seem overwhelming. I begin to act like the other Israelites who were dismayed and terrified of fighting the giant. When Goliath came out, they all ran from him with great fear. (See I Samuel 17.) If I continue to look on these giants with my human eyes, I become defeated and discouraged.

Praise God there is another way! David didn't see the huge, immovable giant. He saw an enemy of the Lord. He knew that God was bigger than anything. He fought the giant with a tiny stone and faith in a big God. He was fighting in the power of the God of Israel. David said to Saul, *"The LORD who delivered me from the paw of the lion and the paw of the bear will deliver me from the hand of this Philistine"* (1 Sam 17:37). David acknowledged who the deliverer was. He knew who to put his trust in. He spoke a statement of faith in the Deliverer. God defeated Goliath using David's small slingshot because David was faithful to do his part.

I, like David, have a choice. Am I going to run away in terror or am I going to stand in the strength of the Lord? The Lord has done so many miraculous deliverances in my life, yet with each new giant, I have a tendency to forget what He has already done. Like David, I can make a statement of faith. "The Lord has delivered me from anxiety and depression before; He will defeat this anxiety, too!" It is amazing what a statement of faith can do when I feel overwhelmed and helpless. When my eyes are off the magnitude of the situation, and onto the magnitude of God's promise of deliverance, there is hope! I have to do my part by standing against the lies of the enemy.

God, You are greater than ALL my enemies. You are using what they mean for harm for good in my life! Praise Your Name!

CLEARLY FOCUSED
NOVEMBER 1997

Things are not very clear for me this month. I must not be sitting with Christ *in the heavenly realms* (Ephesians 2:6) right now. I have been off schedule with my quiet times with the Lord lately. It sure affects my whole life when I don't take the time to spend with Him. My focus is on the situation at hand instead of living above my circumstances. I confess this to the Lord and ask Him to forgive me.

A church leader once told us, "Our circumstances are the harness of God." When I am in the middle of a trying situation, the harness is very restricting and I cry out to the Lord and say, "Get me out of this, Lord. I can't handle it!" But He gently takes me in His arms and says, "My child, I love you. I am not through with you yet. Hang in there! This is for your own good even if it looks like too much. You have much to learn from Me. Let Me teach you what you need to learn to function in the role I have called you to. Trust Me. I am in control and I will never leave you or forsake you."

Submitting to the Lord and what He wants to teach me is not easy. When I do, it removes the fog and lets me see things clearly. I no longer look at them with my human eyes but I see them through God's eyes and they look totally different. No longer is my thinking clouded by my human reasoning. I can rest in the Lord's wisdom and sovereignty and allow Him to do the work He wants to do in my life. Then I can *trust in the Lord with all (my) heart and lean not to (my) own understanding. In all (my) ways acknowledge Him and He will make (my) paths straight* (Proverbs 3:5,6).

YOKES AND BURDENS
DECEMBER 1997

"Come to me, all you who are weary and burdened, and I will give you rest. Take my yoke upon you and learn from me, for I am gentle and humble in heart, and you will find rest for your souls. For my yoke is easy and my burden is light" (Matthew 11:28-30)

There are times when I lay down at night and can't drift off to sleep. My mind is racing with all the burdens of the day. I have to get up out of bed and go journal for a while. As I'm writing, I'm asking the Lord what it is that I can't lay down and let go. Usually something comes to mind right away and I pray, "Jesus, I give you _____. I have been carrying it around on my shoulders when it isn't mine to carry. I lay it at your feet."

Sometimes I have three or four things I've been carrying that are not what the Lord wants me to carry. As I pray, I feel those burdens falling off. I can usually go right to sleep afterward.

Jesus said His yoke is easy and His burden is light. I know when I am carrying more than Jesus wants me to carry when my burden is too heavy and the yoke pulls really hard. Most of the stuff I carry around and worry about and try to figure out is not mine to carry. When I release it to the Lord, the pressure is off of me and onto those shoulders that were meant to carry it. Jesus works miracles in situations that look impossible to me when I give up my striving and place them in His capable hands.

Jesus, I come to you for the rest that my soul needs. I know You will give me rest. I take Your yoke that is easy and Your burden that is light. I leave my own burdens and yokes at the cross. I trust You. I know You will work it all out for my good. Amen.

Reflections
IN THE VALLEY

NEW YEAR, NEW THINGS

JANUARY 1998

*See, the former things have taken place, and **new** things I declare; before they spring into being I announce them to you.* (Isaiah 42:9).

*Forget the former things; do not dwell on the past. See, I am doing a **new** thing! Now it springs up; do you not perceive it?* (Isaiah 43:18-19)

I believe this coming year will be a year of **new** things that God is bringing on this land. I believe that He is speaking these **new** things to His prophets now and will continue to tell us of **new** things He is going to do in His church and in His people. Are we ready for the **new** things He is going to do?

Both these verses call for us to forget the former things. Are we dwelling in the past? Is there pain and heartache in the past that is keeping us from moving forward into the future with the Lord? God will take us back to that pain and heartache and help us walk through it with His agape love. He will help us forgive the persons who hurt or wronged us. He will help us to be able to move ahead without dwelling on the past. Jesus came to set us free from the things that bring us down. Let's open our hearts to Him to do the things that He wants to do.

Let us be open to hear what God is saying to us. He will take us through **new** things one step at a time. He will help us prepare for the **new** things He wants to do in and through His people. Let us be open to how He wants to do it and go with God as He moves forward! Let's not miss it because we didn't perceive it!

SUFFERING WITH A PURPOSE

FEBRUARY 1998

*Praise be to the God and Father of our Lord Jesus Christ, the Father
of compassion and the God of all comfort, who comforts us in all our
troubles, so that we can comfort those in any trouble with the comfort
we ourselves have received from God* (2 Corinthians 1:3-4).

Jesus brought me through a lot of pain and suffering in my lifetime. While
I was going through it I wanted to die. It was very hard to cope. Now
Jesus is using the same painful times to comfort others. Through the things
that I have suffered God wants me to speak to others about the hope and
future He brings. My suffering was for a purpose.

Are you going through a tough time right now? Does it seem like there
is no hope? Does your future look very glum? God is bringing you through
this for a purpose. Right now that doesn't help much, but later on you will
see God's purpose in it all. I never wanted to go through depression and
despair. Now because of going through it I can tell others they are going to
make it. Jesus is real! He cares for us all the time. In our hopelessness, He
offers hope. In our despair, He offers delight, joy, and confidence. In our
pain, He offers comfort. God will bring you to the place where you will be
able to help others because of the miracle in your life.

Have you come through a situation that was painful? Do you have victory? Share that with other people. God will bring others into your life and
across your path that need to hear what you have been through. There is a
reason for the pain and there is a future in sharing what God has done in
your life.

God has truly comforted me during the pain in my life through Himself,
my husband, and other Christians. Without God in my life, I would never
have made it. Now He is leading me to share what He has done to help
others through similar situations. You have been through different pain and
difficulties and you can reach people I could never reach. As we all work together, the kingdom of God will be extended throughout this land.

SPURRING EACH OTHER ON TO GOOD WORKS

MARCH 1998

Hebrews 10:23-25 says, "Let us hold unswervingly to the hope we profess, for He who promised is faithful. And let us consider how we may spur one another on toward love and good deeds. Let us not give up meeting together, as some are in the habit of doing, but let us encourage one another—and all the more as you see the Day approaching."

I am thinking of ways to "spur one another on toward love and good deeds." One way is for us to hear from others who are doing the love and good deeds. This helps us see that God uses ordinary people in their ordinary lives to bring "out-of-the-ordinary" results.

God is faithful! He will fulfill His promises! Let us not be discouraged. We are on the winning team! God is victorious! We need only to do what He tells us to do. The results are totally God's responsibility. As we meet together, let us encourage each other in the things the Lord is doing in our lives. Is God leading you in any way that would be an encouragement to the body of Christ and spur us on to love and good deeds? Then share it with others. We all need that encouragement to get moving with the Lord and not stay stuck in one place. Let's encourage one another in the Lord!

"YOU GIVE THEM SOMETHING TO EAT"

APRIL 1998

*As evening approached, the disciples came to him and said, "This is a remote place, and it's already getting late. Send the crowds away so they can go to the villages and buy themselves some food." Jesus replied, "They do not need to go away. **You give them something to eat.**" "We have here only five loaves of bread and the two fish," they answered. "Bring them here to me," he said. And he directed the people to sit down on the grass. Taking the five loaves and two fish and looking up to heaven, he gave thanks and broke the loaves. **Then he gave them to the disciples, and the disciples gave them to the people.** They all ate and were satisfied, and the disciples picked up twelve basketfuls of broken pieces that were left over* (Matthew 14:15-20).

As I was reading this today, the words of Jesus, "*You give them something to eat*" really stood out to me. Here was a massive problem: feeding five thousand people. No one in their right mind would suggest that five loaves and two fish would feed this crowd. Yet Jesus was asking them to feed the multitude with these meager provisions. When they gave the meager provisions to Jesus, there was more than enough to feed all the people. Would I have given Jesus my meager loaves and fish or would I have argued with Him saying, "This will never feed this many people, Jesus! What are you thinking? There is no way to do that!"

It is the same way in prayer. We come to Jesus with meager faith, only the size of a mustard seed. We pray believing that Jesus can multiply our efforts to be more than enough. All He asks is for us to give it to Him—give Him our meager human provision. He will bless it and it will be more than enough to satisfy the multitudes! We must give all we have to Jesus. We must have faith that Jesus can take all that we have and make it complete and then some! Amazingly, He gives it back to us to do the work He's called us to do.

This month as we focus on prayer, let's remember that all we need and more is in Jesus. All we have to do is ask and believe and He will do great things in our lives!

THE ENEMY HAS NO POWER
MAY 1998

"About judgment, because the ruler (prince) *of this world* [satan] *is judged* **and** *condemned* **and** *sentence already is passed upon him"* (John 16:11 AMP).

"His intent was that now, through the church, the manifold wisdom of God should be made known to the rulers and authorities in the heavenly realms" (Ephesians 3:10).

Satan is condemned and his sentence is already passed upon him. He has no power over us unless we give it to him. We are to make known to the rulers and authorities in the heavenly realms (satan and his demons) that they are defeated; the victory is won! Praise the Lord!

I have often forgotten this. I let myself be pulled down by satan's lies that say I am worthless. All I have to do is tell him, "Satan, get thee behind me! You are defeated! Jesus did the work on Calvary and it is finished! Complete. Your hold on me is broken in Jesus' Name!"

It's already completed. We must enforce it. I can pray with more confidence knowing that I am a representative of Jesus Christ on this earth. I am to present this victory again.

"An understanding of this pattern is crucial, for our intercession is but an extension of the life and ministry of Jesus, as His was of the Father." (Taken from the *Lightning of God* by Dutch Sheets, p. 10.)

LET'S DECLARE THE VICTORY!!
Light the Nation Conference
JUNE 1998

In May 1998, I attended the Light the Nation Conference in Dallas, Texas. It was unlike any conference I have ever been to. The minute the Argentine leaders were introduced, I could tell there was a difference in them. They came on stage and knelt down in humility (ending up on their faces before us and God) thanking us for sending missionaries to Argentina, without whom there would be no revival there. They repented of the way they had treated those first missionaries. I was amazed and awed at the humility that they demonstrated.

There are so many things that happened there that it is hard to choose among them, but here are two sessions that really spoke to me.

Sergio Scataglini's workshop, "How to Keep the Fire"
These are the things he said would help us keep the fire:

1. Believe that the Lord has called you to be completely pure. Ninety-eight percent purity is not enough!
2. Keep giving away the anointing. The Dead Sea is dead because the salt has nowhere else to go. We are the salt of the earth. Don't keep it in and become dead!
3. Flee from immorality—run! You may not look very dignified when you flee but do it anyway!
4. Get close to anointed people.

He talked about his fight with depression and how someone told him not to accept depression as his companion. He put a sign on his dorm room that said, "In the name of Jesus, I will not accept depression in my life!"

Roger Mitchell (from England)'s session on familiar spirits
He identified familiar spirits after saying that England is the father of our nation, and God is turning father nations' hearts to their children nations. The main familiar spirit he emphasized was the exclusive spirit and the attitude that goes with it: "Children should be seen and not heard." He said our

attitudes about children show our hearts. Jesus called children to Him! Roger said it is exclusiveness to leave them out of what God is doing.

Something broke in me as he talked about this spirit and I wept for the rest of his talk. I repented of sharing in this spirit and renounced this spirit from my past. I wept for the hurt it has caused the members of the church I grew up in. I repented of the hurt I have caused with the "holier than thou" attitude that goes with it.

Jesus, you are calling the nations together in unity! Having an exclusive spirit goes contrary to what you are doing in the church. I repent of this attitude and the pride that goes with it. Jesus, I humble myself before you. I commit to raising my children with the right attitude. I will not let my pride get in the way of "training them in the way they should go." I renounce the controlling spirit I have had over them and release them into all you have for them as I "raise them up in the nurture and admonition of the Lord."

This conference was worth all the sacrifice it took to get there. God has touched me deeply! As one of the speakers from Argentina, Claudio Freidzon, said, "Leave the place of 'I can't do that!' Don't be satisfied with the old place. If you want God to bless you, you have to move!"

INTERCESSORY PRAYER
JULY 1998

What is God up to these days? He is bringing intercessory prayer into the forefront. He is giving it the place it needs in revival. I see Him moving across the nation with prayer movements. God is bringing us to our knees and bringing the importance of prayer into view. When we say, "All I can do is pray" we are saying that we can do the most important thing. If we only knew what happens in the heavenlies when we pray and the way the path is cleared for God to work when we intercede for others, we would pray more earnestly and give prayer its proper place of importance.

As God raises up intercessors and the strategic, concentrated prayer, He is raising up warriors to do the battle. We do not fight against flesh and blood but against principalities and powers of this dark age. When we clear the heavenlies, God's work can move through like a child sliding down a slide at the park on wax paper. When a child sits on the paper, he moves with speed because the friction is gone. When we pray, the friction leaves and we can slide through to God's will.

Prayer has become very important to me since going through *The Lightning of God* video series by Dutch Sheets. I had felt like my prayers were not effective and thus had gotten discouraged in praying. After going through this series, I can pray more effectively and strategically. Dutch Sheets gave me confidence in my prayers. This is a whole teaching on why God uses people to bring about His plan in the first place and what intercession really means. I would recommend this series for anyone who is interested in praying more effectively. The book, *Intercessory Prayer* by Dutch Sheets, goes along with the series.

God is raising up His warring army through intercession. I don't want to miss my place in the battle because I'm not prepared. I want to re-present the victory that has already been won. I want to bring people to unity with God and disunity with satan. Praise the Lord! I have seen God work mightily on behalf of a praying small group. I want to stand in the gap for others and see the Lord move mightily in their lives! Will you join me?

WAITING IS NOT EASY
AUGUST 1998

I've been in God's waiting room for a long time. I keep thinking I'm out of it and then God shows me that I'm still here. I feel like I've been in this waiting room forever. I keep pushing my way. The Lord is teaching me to trust that His way is the best way. I always think I know the way and start walking my way and find myself back in the waiting room again.

I have a hard time waiting. When I get a plan in my head I want to move on it now. I don't want to wait. I have gotten into trouble a lot of times because I didn't think it through. God gave me the best husband He could have given me for this waiting stuff because he thinks things through and wants to wait and pray about it before we move forward. I have been very pushy in our marriage. He is the brakes for me. He has helped me stop and think it through. I haven't always appreciated his help, though! (That's an understatement!) I have been sulky and withdrawn because he hasn't agreed with me. Jesus is teaching me that this is very wrong! We need to work together and be in agreement before we move forward.

This is what I feel the Lord saying to me: *"My child, I am gently leading you on a path where you are learning much. Sometimes learning can be painful. Remember that your mistakes don't stop My plan. I can redeem any situation. Just be real. Be open about what you did wrong and don't try to hide it. Through you I am teaching others what it means to WAIT on me! Waiting is the longest step. Remember Moses, Joseph, and Paul. They all had to wait. Moses tried to bring about the deliverance of Israel without Me and ended up fleeing for his life. My ways are far above your ways. Waiting is the time when I refine you to learn to follow Me without question, knowing that I see more than you do. I know what I am doing in your life. The refining part is where you will come out shining like gold but shining for Me and not for yourself. Trust Me to refine all the dross and bring you shining into the future I have for you. Wait! Wait! Wait! My waiting room is a time of seeking Me and learning to hear My voice clearly. Be open to Me and don't shut Me out. Prepare yourself for what is ahead by seeking My face. Seek Me and I will show you the plans I have for you. It is worth waiting for!"*

LEAVING THE FAMILIAR BEHIND
SEPTEMBER 1998

"The watchmen shout and sing with joy, for before their very eyes they see the LORD bringing His people home to Jerusalem. Let the ruins of Jerusalem break into joyful song, for the LORD has comforted His people. He has redeemed Jerusalem. The LORD will demonstrate His holy power before the eyes of all the nations. The ends of the earth will see the salvation of our God. Go now, leave your bonds and slavery. Put Babylon behind you, with everything it represents, for it is unclean to you. You are the Lord's holy people. Purify yourselves, you who carry home the vessels of the LORD. You will not leave in a hurry, running for your lives. For the LORD will go ahead of you and the God of Israel will protect you from behind. See, my servant will prosper; he will be highly exalted" (Isaiah 52:8-13 NLT).

Oh, Jesus! Am I willing to leave behind that which is familiar to move on to Jerusalem? Even though I am in bondage and slavery, it is all I have known. Jesus, show me what this bondage and slavery is really about that I may see that it isn't good for me and isn't where You want me. Help me to move forward into what You have for me in Jerusalem, the city of our God. I want to follow, yet the bondage and slavery to self has been such a part of my life that I don't know if I can leave it. Jesus, bring me out of this bondage. Yes, I will praise You! I will trust You. I will know that You lead me into a place so glorious that it doesn't even compare to where I have been. I let go of what has held me back and move forward into the new place, into the new Jerusalem.

I will listen to the watchmen on the wall. They are telling me that deliverance is near and that the Lord is bringing salvation. I will choose the way of the Lord, even though it is new and unfamiliar. I will choose the new path, forsaking the familiar, and walk into the glorious presence of the Almighty God. I will purify myself from all bondage and slavery and carry home the vessels to Jerusalem. The Lord will protect me from behind, from going back into slavery again and He will prosper me and set me in the proper place. This won't be a place I have striven for, but the place in the body of Christ where I fit. Praise His holy name!

ANXIETY RETURNS!

NOVEMBER 1998

"Do not be anxious about anything, but in everything, by prayer and petition, with thanksgiving, present your requests to God. And the peace of God, which transcends all understanding, will guard your hearts and minds in Christ Jesus" (Philippians 4:6-7).

I truly enjoyed our Ladies Retreat this year. I went there feeling like I didn't need anything specific from the Lord. I felt I was there to support others whom the Lord wanted to touch in a special way. At other retreats, I have received significant healing for myself. This time I was looking forward to seeing God move in others.

I have always had much trouble sleeping at the retreat. This year on Friday evening I slept well. It was later than I usually get to bed but I felt rested in the morning. I didn't try and take a nap in the afternoon because I usually can't sleep anyway and it hinders my sleep at night.

Saturday evening I was a "catcher," helping the speaker minister to people. We stayed downstairs for ministry until 11:30. Then I stayed up with the rest of my roommates until 1 a.m. When I got to bed, I couldn't sleep. I felt the anxious stomach churning all night long. Finally at 2:30 I got up and went into the lounge and wrote in my journal. Around 3 a.m. I laid down on the couch in the lounge and to my surprise, went right to sleep. The next morning after I told them I couldn't sleep, my roommates asked if I wanted prayer for sleeplessness and anxiety. I told them I didn't really need any. I was sure this was only a one night incident. They had ministered to me before for anxiety.

Sunday night at home I was filled up with anxiety and couldn't go to sleep. Things were different for me in that I now had a job to go to on Monday morning. My mind filled with anxious thoughts and my stomach was tied in knots. I worried about everything there was to worry about. I tried journaling, speaking against anxiety, declaring things to satan, and all the other things that had worked before. It was again 3 a.m. when I went to sleep. I woke up at 6 a.m. and that was it. I couldn't sleep anymore. I called a friend and had her pray with me so that I could be rid of anxiety.

I went to work, knowing that if I stayed home with my own thoughts, I would be worse. It was a long, tiring day. I was so glad that my job is very simple. I could do it without much concentration. That evening at small group, I asked for prayer. As they laid their hands on me and prayed, I could feel the anxiety lift right there. That evening I went to sleep almost right way with no anxiety!

The Lord brought to mind a prophetic word He had given me earlier this year. As I re-read it, I knew it was true. I give God all the glory for what He has brought me through and where He is taking me. As you read the following word, think about how the Lord is working in your own life. He is speaking to you, too.

"My daughter I love you! I gave myself for you! Be strong in me. Do not waver or faint. I am with you. Follow Me no matter how things look. I am leading you into green pastures. Each thing that happens is for your strengthening. Each thing that happens is for your good. You are being tested to bring out the gold. Let the dross go. It isn't of any use in My kingdom! I am refining you. Remember how weak you were and how strong you are now? **I have taken you through the valley to strengthen you for the next valley. It will not be as bad. You will not sink as low. I am with you always!! I will never leave you nor forsake you. I am taking you from strength to strength.** *Stand firm then and do not be yoked again with the yoke of slavery! Satan's power is defeated. Stand up and fight him! Be on the offensive. Use your sword! IT IS WRITTEN! I am the Way, the Truth, and the Life. No man comes to the Father but by Me! Come to Me! I will show you the way to the Father!"*

We truly do not have to be anxious about anything. God is working in our lives and He is bringing us through struggles to make us stronger. Stand firm in your faith! God is on the move. Let Him do the work He needs to do to bring you into greater freedom and healing.

GOD'S PURPOSES AND PRIORITIES
FOUND in the "IF's" and "THEN's" of ISAIAH 58
DECEMBER 1998

If you:

- Loose the chains of injustice,
- Untie the cords of the yoke,
- Set the oppressed free,
- Break every yoke,
- Share food with the hungry,
- Provide shelter for the wanderer,
- Clothe the naked,
- Do away with the yoke of oppression by not breaking the Sabbath (which, according to this chapter, is not doing what you please on God's Holy day).
- Call the Sabbath a delight.

Then:

- Your light will break forth like the dawn.
- Your righteousness will go before you.
- Healing will quickly appear.
- The glory of the Lord will be your rear guard.
- The Lord will answer your call.
- When you cry for help, He will say, "Here I am."
- Your light will rise in darkness.
- Your night will become like noonday.
- The Lord will guide you always.
- The Lord will satisfy your needs in a sun-scorched land (or Y2K crisis).
- He will strengthen your frame.
- You will be a well watered garden; like a spring whose waters never fail.
- Your people will rebuild the ancient ruins and raise up age-old foundations.
- You will find your joy in the Lord.
- He will cause you to ride on the heights of the land and to feast on the inheritance of your father Jacob.

These go along with Matthew 6:33, *"But seek first His kingdom and His righteousness* (the first list) *and all these things* (the second list) *will be given to you as well."* This list helps me to see God's heart so I know when I am looking at things from His perspective and when I'm walking in my own way. I hope it helps you, too, as you seek to follow God's purposes and priorities in your life.

35

Reflections
ON THE MOUNTAIN PEAKS

LOOK WHAT GOD HAS DONE!

A new year is here. It is time to reflect on what God has done in the past year and look forward to what God wants to do in the New Year.

This past year has been a year of coming to know the Lord in a new way. I have found a quiet trust in the Lord this year. He is trustworthy and all things work together for good when I trust Him.

Last January, I gave my first "talk" about how God has brought me out of depression. The rest of the year I have been in a series of tests to find out if I really trust Him. Each test has been easier to get through. Each time I don't go as far down. I am thankful for my small group members who have truly been there for me as I struggle with anxiety. I am being refined so that I can say without a doubt that Jesus is my all in all.

God has led me to a couple of books that have really helped me in this new trust. One is the book, *Boundaries*, by Henry Cloud and John Townsend. This book has helped me define how to set those boundaries so I don't do more than I can handle. I learned it is okay to say no. It has brought me freedom in my life. It also helped me in respecting the boundaries of others, especially my husband's. I recommend this book to anyone struggling with saying yes to too many things.

The second book is *The Weigh Down Diet* by Gwen Shamblin. It is more than a diet. In fact, it isn't even a diet; it's a way of life. It's putting God first and breaking free from bondage in our lives. I would recommend this book—or better yet The Weigh Down Workshop—to anyone who is struggling with any type of addiction in their lives.

I also had two freedom ministry sessions this year which brought more freedom. I am beginning to grasp the love the Father has lavished on me that I can be called a "son" of God. I am loved completely and don't have to prove anything to God for Him to love me. He loved me before I ever loved Him. There is nothing I can do to change His love for me. Because of the love God has for me, I can trust Him completely with every aspect of my life! Praise the Lord!

WHAT KIND OF LOVE IS GOD'S KIND OF LOVE?

FEBRUARY 1999

What do we know about the love that comes from above? How can we tell the difference between this love and human love? Let's go on a "tour" of the scriptures to see what this love is all about.

- **God's love is unfailing** (Exodus 15:13). God's love never stops. He will love us always. It isn't dependent on our actions or how we return that love. It will never fail.

- **God's love is slow to anger** (Exodus 34:6). He will be gracious and compassionate and slow to anger. This doesn't say that He will never get angry, but He is slow to that anger.

- **God's love doesn't leave the guilty unpunished** (Numbers 14:18). His love isn't without justice. It doesn't mean we can get away with anything we want, but it does mean that we will be treated with the justice unlike any justice we have witnessed among humans.

- **God keeps a covenant with those who love Him** (Deuteronomy 7:9). He will always keep His covenant. He doesn't say something and then take it back. When God makes a covenant, it stands for a thousand generations to those who love Him. You can depend on Him keeping His side of the covenant.

- **God's love is a saving love** (Psalm 17:7). He will be there as a refuge from enemies for those who love Him. We can come to Him and He will save us. His protection is always there for us who love Him and keep His commandments.

- **God's love makes us alive in Him** (Ephesians 2:4-5). Even while we were dead in our sins, God's love made us alive through Jesus Christ. At our worst, He is there to pick us up and show us mercy.

Are you beginning to get a picture of how great this love is? When we show this kind of love, it will bring great fruit for His kingdom. Love doesn't always mean doing something for someone else. Sometimes the most loving thing we can do is let someone face the consequences of their actions, especially when dealing with our children. The most loving thing God did for King David was to send the prophet Nathan to him to show him his grave sin. We must always seek God to find out what His will is for the person we are relating to and not just do for them what we would see as the most loving.

Celebrate God's love today. How can you and I show God's love more fully? John 13:35 says, *"By this all men will know that you are my disciples, if you love one another."* Let's show the world that we are His disciples!

JESUS' LETTER TO THE PRESENT DAY CHURCH

MARCH 1999

When Jesus wrote the letters to the churches in Revelation, he told them their strengths and then showed them what needed to be changed. What would he say to our congregations? What things are we doing right? What things would he hold against us?

I was impressed with the letter to the church at Laodicea. (Revelation 3:14-22) Jesus gave them some very strong words about how they were neither cold nor hot. He was about to spit them out of his mouth. He also said they thought they were rich, yet they were wretched, pitiful, poor, blind, and naked.

But he doesn't leave them there in their sins. Praise the Lord! The next few verses are so encouraging. *Those whom I love, I rebuke and discipline. So be earnest, and repent. Here I am! I stand at the door and knock. If anyone hears my voice and opens the door, I will come in and eat with him and he with me. To him who overcomes, I will give the right to sit with me on my throne, just as I overcame and sat down with my Father on his throne. He who has an ear, let him hear what the Spirit says to the churches* (Revelation 3:19-22).

No matter what we hear from the Lord about our past sins, mistakes and omissions, Jesus is standing at the door to our hearts, waiting for us to open the door by repenting and turning from our sins. Then we can sit down with him and eat with him. He isn't letting us off the hook, but he isn't leaving us either. He is always there to knock on the door and ask us to come and fellowship with him.

My desire is to see our congregations go forward into all that God has for us. Sometimes we need to look back and turn from our past sins to be able to walk forward. May God grant us the ability to truly look at ourselves as he sees us.

OPENING OUR SPIRITUAL EYES
APRIL 1999

I want to share with you a dream I had a few weeks ago. It is a warning to us. We need to wake up and see things that the Lord wants us to see. I share this dream and give each of you the opportunity to take it before the Lord and ask Him what He wants you to see through it.

I was in a city that was having an earthquake. Our building was damaged and we had to flee. We found a place to stay in the basement of a house that wasn't damaged. We had stayed upstairs. When we saw the owners coming back, I ushered the kids into the basement, hushing them so that we weren't found out. When everything was calm, I went outside to explore. I walked through the streets where tall buildings were leaning a little. I wondered if it was safe to walk there, but no one else seemed concerned. People seemed to be going back to business as usual.

I walked past a multi-level motel building where bodies were hanging out of floors that had collapsed on top of other floors. No one was cleaning it up. I wondered why they acted like it wasn't damaged. I wondered why they didn't take care of the bodies. People around me assured me that things were safe. They didn't even act like anything was out of the ordinary. Everyone was going about their business like everything was normal. It felt like I was the only one who saw the danger of the buildings coming down and the bodies lying around. Then I heard a cracking sound. I realized the motel building was coming crashing down. I ran for my life. I finally realized I couldn't out-run it and lay down with my hands over my head. Amazingly, I didn't get hurt but woke up really shaken.

My cry since this dream has been that the Lord will show me what it is I am not seeing. Bring it to my attention, Lord, the things that I am missing because I'm not in tune with You. Thank you, Jesus, for giving us warnings. Tune my heart to Your heart, Oh Lord, that I may follow where You lead.

THE RESULTS ARE UP TO THE LORD!

MAY 1999

The other day I was seeking the Lord for my neighbor who is going through an intensely painful period in her life. I was feeling overwhelmed with the pain and anguish she is experiencing. As I sought the Lord about this situation I sensed Him saying: *Cry out to Me for those around you who are hurting. Don't try to do anything on your own. I have a plan for each person you are relating to that includes more people than just you. You need to do your part. You don't have to make things happen. Just be open to listen to My voice. When I say move, move. When I say speak, speak. And when I say pray, pray. I am continually looking for people who will go when I say go and stay when I say stay. Open those clogged ears and listen to My voice. Don't question Me, just do it! I have higher plans than you have and My ways don't look like your ways. Trust Me and move ahead when the cloud moves. Stand still when the cloud stands still. Walk in My path and listen to Me.*

As I seek His face for those around me, I don't have to feel overwhelmed. I can do what He's asking me to do and leave the results up to Him. He will do the work. All I have to do is bring her needs before Him and allow Him to work in her life. There are some things I can do for her that may help alleviate some pain, but mostly all I can do is pray. It was comforting for me to know that the results are in His hands. I just need to listen to His voice and follow the path He places before me. That seems much less of a burden to me.

The next time I feel overwhelmed, I will remember this word. I will put the person or situation into His strong arms of love, and let Him be the one who carries the burden.

THE ENEMY HAS NO AMMUNITION IN HIS GUN!!

JUNE 1999

The other night I had a vivid dream. Faith rose up in me when I woke up. There is no ammunition in the enemy's gun! Fear and intimidation are his only tactics against us! Here is the dream as I remember it:

It was awful! The Nazis were everywhere. I could go about my regular routine except once in a while a Nazi official would be wheeled up to me in a wheelchair. The guy pushing him would carry a small pistol, pointed at me. The guy in the wheelchair was covered with a blanket. The blanket had a Nazi emblem on it. He wore a Nazi uniform. He had on shades and a Nazi hat so I could never see his face.

Sometimes the guy in the wheelchair was just an ordinary soldier. I had absolutely no fear. I wasn't intimidated with a regular soldier. But when it was this Nazi official I was much more intimidated. He would be wheeled up to me and I would be given orders. I wouldn't be fearful but I wouldn't talk back. I would receive the orders and do them.

The last time when this official was wheeled up to me, he ordered me to say, "Hail, Hitler!" before I carried out his orders. I knew I couldn't do that so I totally refused, then turned and ran. The one pushing the wheelchair shot me with his gun before I got very far. I fell to the ground believing I was dying. I couldn't feel any pain but figured I was too badly wounded to feel pain anymore. Shots kept coming as I was lying there. I decided that if I appeared dead, they would give up and go away. But then I would move a bit or twitch, and they would shoot again.

Finally I realized, to my surprise, that the gunshots were not hurting me at all. I was only feeling a force like a blow without pain which would make my body move a little. When they were gone, I got up and went about my business, this time knowing they were powerless against me!

I woke up singing, "I went to the enemy's camp and took back what he stole from me!" The enemy uses fear and intimidation to keep us from the realization that his guns have no ammunition! When someone isn't afraid, he has no power at all! So we have nothing to fear! His weapons have no ammunition! We can get up after an attack and go about our business, not hurt at all!

FORGIVENESS ISN'T EASY BUT THE REWARDS ARE GREAT!

JULY 1999

After doing the sermon on unforgiveness, I have been tested in this area. I realize now that I can never sit back and say that I have arrived and am now totally "unforgiveness-free!" There are many times when I know that I shouldn't be acting this way. I should forgive. But my flesh wants the other person to suffer a little first.

I was very upset with my husband. I went into my "prayer closet" and poured out my heart to the Lord about what he did that upset me so much. (It was the same old issue surfacing again—the house.) As I was crying out to God, some of my frustration and anger drained away. I then released the situation to Him, giving up the right to control what goes on.

Next I sat down, waiting silently before the Lord as I wrote what I felt God was saying to me. God spoke to me, but He never once told me what Bob should or shouldn't do. Instead He gently showed me what I needed to do. I was to worry about my motives and heart condition and He will worry about my husband's. He didn't even talk about any of the things I had poured out to Him. He turned His searchlight on my heart and showed me what had to go. After that, I could forgive my husband easily.

Sometimes I wonder why God even bothers with us humans. We stumble and fall so often. Just when I think that I am doing well, another roadblock appears and sends me flying. Guess what? It's not in what we can or can't do, it's in who God is and what He has created in us. Humility is to know who to put our confidence in. Will we put it in ourselves and our ability, or will we put it in God who knows the big picture? He always gives us what we need to fulfill the calling He has placed on our lives.

"We must turn to the cross of Jesus to find both the forgiveness and the power to overcome sin," a quote from Rick Joyner's book, *Overcoming the Religious Spirit*. Jesus has the power we need to forgive and be forgiven and to overcome. The freedom that comes is much more wonderful than the feeling of hanging on to the resentment and anger. There is no comparison!

TRASH AND THE LOCAL HOMECOMING FESTIVAL

AUGUST 1999

I enjoyed our outreach very much. It was so neat to see the impact we had by giving out free water and balloons to the people at the homecoming. Some would even come up just to tell us how they appreciated us being there.

On Friday evening we ended up with extra people so our leader got us involved in emptying the trash barrels. A friend and I helped one of the homecoming workers empty the trash bins. He would lift up the heavy barrels while we made sure the trash stayed in the bags. The guy kept thanking us over and over again. It was a very messy job, but it felt so good to know that I was doing something that was greatly appreciated.

On Saturday evening, I noticed that the trash barrels were full and running over. Another friend and I decided to empty them. We went to the first one which had almost as much trash around the barrel as in it. It was in full view of the people standing in line at one of the concessions. Annie and I had a hard time lifting the barrel and getting the trash in the bag. People were watching us and giving us advice as we were struggling with the barrel. We were very glad to get done with that one!

When we approached the next barrel, which was worse than the first one, a lady looked at us and said, "It is about time! People are starting to complain." She said it in a manner that showed her disgust at us for not emptying the barrel sooner. I wanted to tell her that we were just doing a favor to the homecoming committee; that it wasn't my fault that it hadn't been done; that wasn't my responsibility. Instead I just smiled and went on emptying the trash.

I learned a lot about servanthood. There was no way the people in the park could know that I was doing the job as a servant of Jesus Christ just by looking at me. I realized that I enjoy doing things when I can get a pat on the back. It was harder to continue when I knew that people blamed me for the mess. I need to do acts of service whether I get the praise or not!

Matthew 6:1 says, "*Be careful not to do your 'acts of righteousness' before men, to be seen by them. If you do, you will have no reward from your Father in heaven.*" Sometimes I want that recognition from men. But my reward in heaven will be much better than receiving a few "pats on my back" here on earth.

WATER AND THE FAIR PARADE
SEPTEMBER 1999

Picture the hottest day of the year. The sun is beating down. You are so thirsty from the hot, humid weather that your lips are parched and your throat is dry. All you want is water in any form—water for drinking, water for swimming in, water for splashing in, or water for bathing. Now picture someone coming along with small cups of water, passing them out to the many thirsty people around you. You have only a very slight chance of getting any of the tiny amount of water that wouldn't help much anyway.

This was the way it was for people along our 4-H Fair Parade route this year. Our church served cold water from coolers on the back of the pick-up truck we had in the parade. Runners ran from the truck to the crowd with small cups of water.

I was one of the runners. It was very hot. People along the parade route were crying out for the water I held in my hands. They were reaching out their hands saying, "Water, water. May I please have water?" I knew that the tiny bit of water I gave them wasn't enough to quench their thirst, but would help a little against the heat. I also knew we could never get to all the thirsty people. We could only satisfy a small percentage of the demand for water.

Now picture a different scene. You know that if you can just get your hands on this cup, your thirst will be quenched. You are dying of thirst. But all you need is one sip and you will be satisfied. There is plenty to go around. Everyone who wants a drink can have one. People start drinking the water and then passing it on to the next person. Soon wells of water are springing up everywhere you look. There is more water than needed to go around.

Jesus said, "*Everyone who drinks this water will be thirsty again, but whoever drinks the water I give him will never thirst. Indeed, the water I give him will become in him a spring of water welling up to eternal life*" (John 4:13-14).

Jesus satisfies all the thirsty.

I want to continue to give this water that springs up into eternal life to all who drink of it. I want to help get this water out to all I come in contact with. What a picture! Jesus can satisfy every thirsty soul! Praise His name!

GOD TURNS MY VALLEY EXPERIENCES INTO DAYS OF FEASTING!
OCTOBER 1999

Sleeplessness and anxiety have returned! This is the "thorn in the flesh," so to speak, that I struggle with off and on. I had thought I had moved beyond it; that it was a thing of the past. I even told a friend of mine I did not think that I would ever again struggle with anxiety. I told her I may have some sleepless nights, but the anxiety is gone. One week later it was back! Talk about bringing me down. I come to the place where I have to totally trust the Lord for everything, even my very existence. I cannot live without Him. I am nothing on my own. He is my all in all. It humbles me to know that I can have it all figured out and think I can make it through anything and then, wham! I am right back where I started.

During this experience, I thought about the song, "Thank You for the Valley," an old song I learned in childhood.

Thank you for the valley I walked through today
The darker the valley, the more I learn to pray
Thank you for every hill I climbed
For every time the sun didn't shine
Thank you for every lonely night
I prayed till I knew everything was all right
And I thank you for the valley I walked through today

The valley is a place where you can learn things you cannot learn anywhere else. This is true for me. I read Psalm 23:4-5: *Even when I walk through the dark valley of death, I will not be afraid, for you are close beside me. Your rod and your staff protect and comfort me. You prepare a feast for me in the presence of my enemies. You welcome me as a guest, anointing my head with oil. My cup overflows with blessings* (NLT).

As I ponder these verses it causes me to reflect on the fact that when I am anxious, I have a hard time eating. My stomach is upset and churning. This scripture says that in the valley of the shadow of death, the shepherd prepares a feast in front of my enemies. It must be a very peaceful place in order to be

49

able to eat a feast there. I want that peace so my stomach won't be in turmoil, worrying about everything that could happen in the next ten years! I want God to come and be peace to me so I will be able to relax enough to eat in front of my "enemies."

Another thing I notice is that when the shepherd leads me to green pastures and beside quiet waters, He gives nourishment which sustains me, like an "everyday" meal. In contrast, when I go through the "*valley of the shadow of death*," I receive a feast. *The Message* says it is a six-course meal—more than just nourishment and sustenance. It is much more than I need. It is a pleasure meal! This feast is in the valley, in the presence of my "*enemies.*" It ends with my head being anointed with oil and my cup being filled to overflowing with blessings.

When I start down this path to anxiety, I really hate it. I do not want to go through it again. I hate being so vulnerable. But it is in this valley that I receive the feast; the "more than enough" nourishment that sustains me until the next valley. Jesus did not promise me there would be no valleys. What He promises is that He will turn our valleys into the greatest experience of our lives. He promises a place where we are treated as royalty in His kingdom; where we can be an example to our "enemies" showing them we are not going to give up. We receive His anointing and the greatest blessings there. While it does not make me want more valleys to walk through, it does let me know that these times are not wasted. They are used for my good.

It is a great victory when we can be thankful for the valleys! When I look back over the valleys that have come into my life, I know that without them, I would not be where I am today. I learned a lot there "in the presence of my enemies," and am thankful that they were there. I am also thankful that Jesus walked with me through them, fed me richly, anointed my head with soothing ointment, and showered me with blessings.

Jesus, I pray for anyone who is going through a valley right now. I pray they can see You and what You are doing in the valley. I pray they can eat the feast set before them. I pray this will be an experience where the greatest anointing and the greatest blessing come for them. Give them hope today so they can know You are there with them, that Your rod and Your staff are comforting them, and that You will never leave them alone in the valley! I pray this in Jesus' precious name. Amen.

GOD'S TIMING IS PERFECT!
NOVEMBER 1999

I have wanted to move to a bigger house for years. We live in a 1200 square foot house which is crowded with the six of us. There is no living space in the basement, either. It wasn't in very good shape for a while. I wanted to sell it as a "fixer-upper" and move years ago. But the kind of house we could have afforded then wouldn't have improved our situation much at all. My husband always wanted to fix it up and then sell it. Actually for a long time, he didn't want to move at all. I felt that the Lord wanted us to move. But it was hard to truly hear God when my heart was so set on moving. At times I would tell the Lord that I couldn't stand another minute in this house. The winters were especially bad with nowhere to put the extra coats, boots, mittens and hats.

There were a few significant things that happened in the past year, which helped us in getting our house ready. The first thing was my husband spent a week at home totally gutting and redoing our only bathroom. He did a wonderful job.

During the work on the bathroom, our garage burned down. It was a detached, cement block garage (an eyesore!). We lost some things that were valuable but a lot of it was junk. (Our lawn mower wasn't damaged at all.) We decided not to put up another garage but instead put up a small shed and used the rest of the money from the insurance company to pay off bills and finish fixing up the house. We used some of it for vinyl siding.

Another major thing needed was finishing the upstairs walls which needed patching and painting. The doors and woodwork on the main floor also needed a coat of paint. It seemed like a huge job to us but one very wonderful gentleman from our church painted it for nothing. It was the boost we needed. We are forever grateful to him for his gift to us. The end was in sight!

Next my husband put in a second bathroom off the master bedroom. He was able to get a sink from a job he was working on at the time. A friend gave us the commode. Bob did a wonderful job of making it look very nice.

We signed the papers to put our house on the market on August 21, 1999. On September 21, 1999, we accepted a full-price offer! We ended up with two people making offers on the same night. We found out later that a third person called to make an offer the next day. God is so good!

We had been looking at a particular house in a subdivision for a month or two. The price was higher than we wanted to pay. After we accepted the offer on our house, we made an offer on this all-brick ranch that has lots of room. We were able to buy it for considerably less than the listing price. Praise the Lord! We are moving on October 29, 1999! I still can't believe it!

I thought back to the years of wanting a house and I was convicted of my attitude. I had coveted a new house. My attitude was not right toward my husband. I repented of thinking a house was more important than the Lord and for making life miserable for Bob. As I was weeping before the Lord in repentance, I realized how gracious He is. He provided a much better house than we could have bought even a year ago. He provided all the circumstances to get us to this place. In spite of my sin before Him, He still gave me the desires of my heart. His timing is perfect! Mine was all screwed up! He's never early, never late!

The house is in the same school district for all our kids. It is big enough to have a lot of people over at the same time. There are a lot of bonuses about the house that I wouldn't have even asked for.

After our house was on the market, I asked the Lord if we could at least move before winter. Bob was asking the Lord if we could move by Thanksgiving. When he told me that, I told him that was asking too much! But God moved us almost a month BEFORE Thanksgiving.

My timing would have been awful. We wouldn't have been able to improve our situation by much. Now, He has given us a house far beyond my expectations. I know that this house is for His purposes and He will use it for His glory.

Now to Him who is able to do exceedingly abundantly above all that we ask or think, according to the power that works in us, to Him be glory in the church by Christ Jesus to all generations, forever and ever. Amen (Ephesians 3:20-21 NKJV).

TRADITIONS THAT BRING US TOGETHER
DECEMBER 1999

The Christmas holiday is fast approaching. It seems to be a busy, busy season of running hither and yon without a time to rest. I can get so busy that we forget that the real reason for the season is Jesus coming to earth to take away our sins. I have a few things that we do with our kids each year to help bring the focus back onto Jesus and get the focus away from the commercial aspect of Christmas.

A few years ago, I made an Advent tree out of felt. It was from the book called, *Family Celebrations—Meeting Christ in your Holiday and Special Occasions,* by Ann Hibbard. Each day of Advent, there is a circle to put on the tree. We read a scripture, sing a hymn and talk about that aspect of the Advent season. The first one is a symbol of Alpha and Omega. We read in Revelation 22:13: "*I am the Alpha and the Omega, the First and the Last, the Beginning and the End.*"

It begins with the Alpha and the Omega and moves into Jesus creating all things and then talks about sin and our need for a savior. It looks at the passages in Isaiah that foretell the coming of Jesus. It ends with the wise men coming and worshiping the baby Jesus. The kids love taking turns putting up the circles each day. (They are fastened with Velcro.) We don't always follow the suggestions for songs and prayers but we read the verses and talk about what the picture on the circle symbolizes.

Another thing we do is to make up cheese balls and put them in a tin with some fancy crackers. We make about four or five of them. An evening or two before Christmas Eve, we go to neighbors or friends we especially want to minister to and give them the tin. We usually are invited inside for fellowship with them. I got the idea from a friend. Her family came one year and sang carols to us. They left a basket of goodies with us when they were done. It makes a great connection with people on our "Oikos" list. ("Oikos" refers to our circle of influence. It means "family unit," including extended family and network of relationships.)

I also try and have some kind of Christmas craft for the kids and me to do together. Last year we made popcorn ball snowmen with colored sugar and candy for the decorations. It was fun creating our "snow village." We displayed them on top of the piano in a snowy scene on a cookie sheet.

We started a tradition a couple years ago making egg rolls on Christmas Eve as a family. We make, roll, and fry them together. It has become something we look forward to each year.

We also attend the Christmas Eve service here at church if we can. It is a significant time of worshiping with our church family. The candle-lighting at the end of the service is something we don't like to miss.

Christmas can be the most stressful time of the year. Or it can be a great time of family traditions. I'm sure all of you have traditions that you could share with others. Why don't you take the time to tell someone else some things your family does that keeps the focus on Jesus this season? It would give us all new ideas to try with our families!

Merry Christmas to all!

Reflections
AT UNEXPECTED TURNS

How I Met My Husband

Bob and I met on a youth group bike trip called Out Spokin'. The group drove to Brown County, Indiana in someone's motor home. We biked around Brown County for 2½ days. I was invited by one of my friends who went to Bob's church.

Bob teased me a lot there. The girls in his youth group warned me. "When Bob likes you, he never lets go. Be careful, Marla," they said. Well, I wasn't careful and look what happened!

After we got back from Out Spokin', I didn't see Bob for two weeks. The third Sunday after the trip, I came to his church. I walked into the sanctuary as the Sunday School superintendent opened the lesson. I noticed a man at the pulpit. He wore plaid polyester pants and looked like he was in his thirties. When he started speaking, I realized it was Bob. What a change from the guy who wore short pants and no shirt most of the time during our bike trip! (For the next few birthdays and Christmases, I gave him clothes as a gift!)

He sat with me during the worship service. After church, I waited around, talking to everyone I knew, wanting him to ask me out. I finally gave up and walked to my car. He came running after me (Bob says he walked briskly) and asked me to go with him and the youth group to a restaurant for lunch. We ended up spending the rest of the evening with the youth at his parent's house. On the way home, we had a flat tire! All in all, it was a memorable day.

We were married exactly a year from the day we met. I was only 19 at the time, though I don't recommend getting married that young. I had a lot of growing up to do after we were married. I had all the ideals in my head of how this was going to work and none of them proved true. We weathered many storms our first year of marriage, but it has all been worth it. I'm thankful for a loving husband. I'm glad he never let me go!

SPRING IS AROUND THE CORNER

MARCH 2000

I've been in a winter slump this last month. I didn't feel much like spending time with the Lord. My quiet time with Him was way too quiet. I felt like I was just going through the motions. I had a hard time getting up in the morning and would sleep longer than usual. Life was dull and lifeless. It looked like there wasn't any life at all. How could I go on feeling so barren?

This morning I awoke earlier than normal. I was excited to be able to spend time with God. A newness came over me. I felt hope again. Winter isn't going to last forever, although it feels that way sometimes. I got out of bed this morning anticipating what God had for me.

It has been winter in my life, but spring is around the corner. Spring is when new life comes forth at breakneck speed. Life is in the air. Life is everywhere. I began to thank God for the winter months that give me that anticipation of the new life He is bringing to me. Without the winter months, I wouldn't appreciate the new life that spring brings. There is a reason for every season of life. I sense God's purpose in winter is to help me appreciate His new life in me.

During the "dry" times in my life, I need to remain open to the pruning and breaking that God needs to do. I need to remain in the vine. I need to wait patiently for God to work. I need to see my life the way God sees it and not give in to the lies of the enemy that make me believe there is not hope. God isn't finished with me. I will not be dormant forever. He is preparing me for the next season where new life springs forth.

Lord Jesus, I pray for anyone else who is experiencing a dry time. I pray for a well of living water to spring up in their heart and bring life to their innermost being. I pray that You will give them new hope and new life within. Thank you that everyone who hungers and thirsts will be filled. I ask this in Jesus' precious name. Amen.

STEPS OUT OF THE DARKNESS
APRIL 2000

I have been asked lately how I made it out of anxiety and depression. I decided to write down the steps that helped me recover. There is no one thing that did it. It was a step here and a step there—a process that took a long time. Each time I made it through the anxiety to peace, I got stronger.

For those of you who do not know, I have had several severe anxiety attacks in my lifetime, starting with the birth of my first child. I had not slept for at least 2 or 3 nights and was in a catatonic state when my husband brought me into the hospital. They diagnosed me with Severe Post-partum Depression. I was put on an anti-depressant and was able to barely cope through the next few months. Since then, I have had lots of times of minor anxiety and two other major times of being in that place of shear panic with sleepless, anxiety-filled nights.

These steps helped me find freedom, but are not necessarily in sequential order:

- **Getting help**: In severe cases this help should be in the form of medical attention as it was for me the first time when Bob finally realized that I wasn't going to get better and put me in the hospital. In minor cases it has been as simple as finding someone to pray with me. I had a lot of friends around me who told me that I could call them anytime day or night if I needed them. They were a big help to me.

- **People telling me I was going to make it**: "You can get through this, Marla. I know you can!" I was usually at a place where I believed I would never get better and those words penetrated deeply and brought hope.

- **Speaking out against the lies of the enemy**: I would do this by saying the declaration printed below, given to me by my pastor. Sometimes I would have to get out of bed in the middle of the night and go somewhere that I wouldn't disturb those who were sleeping and say this declaration out loud so that the enemy would hear it.

  In faith, I claim for my mind and my emotions the full deliverance and freedom accomplished by Jesus on the cross of Calvary.

I refuse to accept the negative and improper thoughts that satan would try to put in my mind. I have the mind of Christ, according to your Word.

I choose to take my mind from the sphere of satan and place it in the realm of the Holy Spirit of God and I yield my mind and my will only to the Living God.

Satan, your hold on my mind is broken.

I thank you, Jesus, for You are my deliverance and my freedom.

- **Telling myself the truth**: I would have to tell myself that I could make it through the next day even if I didn't get any sleep at all. I had a fear after the first depression that whenever I could sleep I was okay but when I couldn't, I needed help. Whenever I would have anxiety and couldn't sleep, I made it so much worse by having fear that I would go down that same road as before. Fear of fear is how Dr. Hart puts it in his new book, The Anxiety Cure. I would have to say, "It doesn't matter if I can't sleep tonight. I've made it through worse nights than this." or "I will be all right tomorrow when the guests come. Even if the house isn't totally clean. It isn't the end of the world. Whatever I can get done, I'll get done. The rest will just have to wait." I would say these things over and over, trying to relax my breathing and give myself a way out. Sometimes I needed Bob to say that he would do whatever it is I was worrying about. That alone would give me peace, even though I didn't really need him to do it. (For me things usually look better in the morning.).

One night I couldn't sleep. There was so much to accomplish the next day. I knew I wouldn't get it all done. I asked Bob to help me. (Of course I woke him up because he usually has no trouble sleeping at night.) He prayed with me and did the usual things. Then he said, "Okay, Marla. This side of the bed is the side of responsibilities." He pounded on my side of the bed. "This side is the side of no responsibilities." He pounded on his side. Then he had me switch sides of the bed and I was able to go right to sleep.

- **Freedom Ministries**: I went through many types of freedom ministry during this time of struggle. It helped me get healing from my past so that I could see things in a different light in the future. One of the ways was to be able to accept God's love for me. I always thought I had to perform a certain way or be "spiritual" enough to receive God's love. Of course I never measured up, so I believed at the emotional level that God didn't love me. (I knew in my mind that God loved me, but my feelings said that he couldn't.) I was able to actually believe in my experiential mind that God loved me just the way I am and that he loves my personality because he created me that way. It changed my life. I was able to stop trying to be somebody I wasn't and be the Marla that God created me to be. What freedom!

- **Journaling really helped**: I started writing a prayer journal in 1995, about nine months before my second major experience. I wrote things in there that I wouldn't be able to tell anyone but God. I would write down my deep feelings knowing that God wouldn't condemn me. He would only gently steer me down the right path. I also learned to write down what I felt God was saying to me. I love to go back and read those words from the Lord and see how God was leading me to health and wholeness.

A NEW LOOK AT THE SONG OF SOLOMON

JUNE 2000

Ever since Jerry Reeder came and spoke at our church, I have been intrigued by his study of the book of Song of Solomon. I have since listened to the tapes from his series called, *Principles from the Song of Solomon* on this "hard to understand" book of the Bible. I never thought of it as pertaining to my walk with the Lord before. I always thought of it in the context of married love.

I realized as I was listening to Jerry's series that I need so much affirmation from God to believe that He **enjoys my company**. When Jerry said that the Lord embraces us in our weaknesses, I started crying because I had felt condemned whenever I knew I wasn't spending time with Him like I should. I have since been trying not to give in to the lies that I have to do something to measure up to God. He enjoys being with me! He doesn't want to be on my list of things to do; He wants me to be with Him without an agenda mapped out for our time together. What an awesome concept that is! The God who created the universe, wants to spend time with me! I can get so overwhelmed with that thought! What a wonderfully great God we serve! Praise His name.

Recently I had a Theophostics Prayer Ministry session where I found God's love for me expressed in a different setting. ("Theo" means "God" and "phostics" means "light." It's the ministry of a Dr. Ed Smith in which one allows God to speak to him or her in a past, painful memory. The whole idea is to bring God's light into that dark event.) In this session I "saw" a picture of myself as a little girl standing and staring at this huge storm that was coming right at me. The fear in me was so overwhelming I wanted to turn and run in the other direction. I was weeping uncontrollably. I saw myself turning and starting to run, yet I felt compelled to stay. It was like I was in the position of running away and Jesus was telling me to stay. I ended up staying but I was very, very scared, crying out, "It's going to swallow me up! I have to run!"

All of a sudden I realized that the storm was over. It hadn't even gotten to me. The clouds were gray yet still and peaceful. I saw myself standing tall and straight. I had such a sense of victory realizing I made it through the storm still standing! It hadn't swallowed me up!

I learned from that experience that I can make it through any of the storms that life brings me. I don't need to turn and run. Jesus loves me and will protect me. I can stand and face whatever comes my way because He promised that He *"is faithful; He will not let you be tempted beyond what you can bear. But when you are tempted, He will also provide a way out so that you can stand up under it"* (1 Cor 10:13). His way out is usually standing up under it, not escaping the trial altogether!

This was another affirmation of God's love for me. He loves me **through the trials. What an awesome God we serve!** Even though we don't always understand His ways, they are always exactly what we need for each situation we face!

Another verse that talks about standing: *Therefore, my dear brothers, **stand firm. Let nothing move you.** Always give yourselves fully to the work of the Lord, because you know that your labor in the Lord is not in vain* (1 Cor 15:58). I pray that I may continually **stand firm** and not let the things that life brings make me falter in the way the Lord has called me.

Remember that God loves you right where you are right now! He wants to show you how much He loves you, too. He wants you to trust Him with all of the situations that come your way.

PERSONAL WORDS FROM THE LORD

JULY 2000

This month I was struggling with what to write. I was browsing through old journal entries and I found three prophetic messages from the Lord that jumped out at me. I hope they encourage you and challenge you as they have encouraged me and challenged me to go higher with the Lord.

April 5, 1999: *My daughter, stand firm. Cry out to Me for those around you who are hurting. Don't try to do anything on your own. I have a plan for each person you are relating to that includes more people than just you. You just need to do your part. You don't have to make things happen. Just be open to listen to My voice and when I say move, move. When I say speak, speak. And when I say pray, pray. I am continually looking for people who will go when I say go and stay when I say stay. Open those clogged ears and listen to My voice. Don't question Me, just do it. I have higher plans than you have and My ways don't look like your ways. Trust Me and move ahead when the cloud moves and stand still when the cloud stands still. Walk in My path and listen to Me.*

May 10, 1999: *My child, I love you. I am doing a work in your heart. You have become strong in Me and able to place things in My hands. You can't carry things that I haven't given you. It will crush you. Let go and let Me do the work I have planned. Let go of the hurts, the offenses, and the unforgiveness. I want to purify your heart. You must give Me permission to do that. It won't be easy. It won't be fun and may be painful, but the end result is freedom and community.*

My body is supposed to work together and complement each other. Instead the hand is telling the foot that it isn't walking right, the arms are trying to work like hands and there is much confusion and strife. Let go of the other person and start looking at your place in the body. Start asking yourself if you are walking in the destiny I have called you. Stop trying to see if everyone else is doing their job right while you are letting yours go. I have placed diversity in My body because it takes all of you to become what I want you to become. Fulfill your functions and encourage others to fulfill their functions. Bring admonition with love. Speak the truth in love. Don't carry other people's boulders. Give them to Me. You were not made to carry it all. That's what the cross is for. I laid down My life to bring freedom to all. Put those burdens at the cross and leave them there. There is hope and healing!

June 21, 2000: My child, I love you. I gave Myself for you. Keep trusting Me. I am not finished with the work I am doing in you. You must daily give your life to Me. You must abandon yourself to Me. Stop putting confidence in who Marla is. Instead put your confidence in who I am in you. I have done a work in you. Tell others what I have done. Don't stop proclaiming My work in you. Be real. Be honest. Don't embellish your life; tell the truth and see how I use what you have gone through to bring healing to others. TRUST is the key. Trust Me in everything you do. Walk in My ways. Speak My words of healing. Today is the day of healing in emotions. Walk upright. Speak truth. Tell what I put on your heart. You are the apple of My eye. Walk in the way I have chosen for you. Stay on the path. Don't try and walk in the flesh. It only bungles everything I am trying to do in you. You can walk in the flesh and have "things." You can walk in the spirit and have "relationships." It's your choice. Choose life and relationships. Nothing else matters!

A TIME OF REST

August 2000

The Lord has been speaking to me about taking time to rest. In this culture, we are so busy. I am no exception. Sometimes I feel like I am on a treadmill going nowhere … fast! I also have a tendency to worry and "stew" about things so that my mind is not at rest, either. This makes for a very hurried life with no time for complete rest.

God established a precedent when He worked for six days and rested the seventh. God doesn't need a day of rest. He isn't subject to being tired. He did this to help us to establish a day of rest. He set up the Sabbath day for us to follow. It is for our own benefit. It shouldn't be used as a "law" or a restriction, but as a way for us to make sure we put a regular time of complete rest in our lives.

What does resting mean? The American Heritage Dictionary gives these meanings for the word "rest": 1) a cessation of work, exertion, or activity; 2) peace, ease, or refreshment resulting in sleep or the cessation of an activity; 3) sleep or quiet relaxation; 4) the repose of death; 5) relief or freedom from disquiet or disturbance; 6) mental or emotional tranquility; 7) termination or absence of motion.

Rest means sleep but it also means quiet relaxation. Can you quiet your mind after a long day of work? When you lay down to sleep, does your mind rest, too? I used to have a lot of trouble with this. Whenever I was in the middle of doing something, I would mull it over in my mind at night and it would disturb my sleep. I have learned that the best way for me to put my mind to rest is to journal all my thoughts and feelings on paper as a prayer to God. This releases all of it in His hands and allows me to rest my mind from worrying about the outcome. Sometimes I need to process something with someone else before I can truly let it go. Bob tells me for every hour of conversation I have, I need ten minutes of processing to let go of it. This might be a little exaggerated, but it has helped if I keep that in mind when I have had a full day of conversation and interaction with people.

The Bible says so much about rest and peace (shalom). Psalm 34:14 says, *"Seek peace and pursue it."* This makes it sound like it isn't something that you can passively receive. Psalm 16:9 says, *"Therefore my heart is glad and my tongue rejoices; my body also will rest secure."* Psalm 62:1,5 says, *"My soul finds rest in God alone; my salvation comes from Him. Find rest, oh my soul, in God alone; my hope comes from Him."* And of course there is the familiar passage in Psalm 91:1: *"He who dwells in the shelter of the Most High will rest in the shadow of the Almighty."* There are many more verses on rest and peace (shalom) but I won't list them all. If you want to do more study, look the verses up in your concordance.

If God is interested in us finding rest and peace, then He is also there to give it to us. He is our provider and He is the God of peace. We can only find true rest in Him alone. There is no other way to have complete peace (shalom) any other way than through Jesus.

Jesus, I thank you for the peace and rest that only comes from You.

OUR GOD IS A PRACTICAL GOD
SEPTEMBER 2000

Bob and I were really struggling with some discipline issues with our children. The main thing was the fighting and bickering among themselves and disrespectful attitudes toward others. We were at our wits end. What ended up happening when they were fighting was that I would get into the fight and end up yelling at them like they were yelling at each other. They would try to tell me who was at fault or who started it and the fighting would escalate with me being involved over my head. I knew this couldn't go on. Something had to happen. I cried out to the Lord to please help us find a solution to break the cycle.

One Saturday morning, I was putting up peaches and listening to Parent Talk Radio. They have a call-in program where parents ask questions and the host, Randy Carlson, answers them. One woman asked what to do with her kids' fighting. Her kids were close to the ages of our three younger kids and she put into words all that I had been struggling with the last few months. I eagerly waited for Dr. Carlson's practical solution.

He said, "When kids fight, they do so for a purpose. They are actually cooperating together to get something when they are fighting." He named a couple of things that they would want to accomplish but one stood out: "Kids fight to get their parents overly involved in their lives." He told the mom who called in that she should sit the kids down and say something like this: "I am no longer going to be judge and jury in your fights. It is for you to work out. If I need to get involved, then you will go to your room or sit on a chair for 30 minutes." He did tell her that she would need to step in if one was really hurting another. He told her that kids need to learn conflict resolution because this is a skill that will be needed throughout life. It is good to give them tools to work out their conflicts but not get involved in being judge and jury.

That evening after the peaches were done, Bob and I sat the kids down and explained that we were no longer going to be involved in their fighting. If they couldn't work it out, all those fighting would end up in their rooms for a half an hour. It has worked like a charm. Now when they tattle all I have to say is, "Are you sure you want me to be involved in this fight?" I have found that the fighting is usually not one-sided but involves more than one person even though one may end up always being the one that hits the other. This has really freed me up and helped me stay calm, not getting into a yelling match with our kids!

The other issue was disrespect. Our kids were getting so disrespectful. When I called them on it, they would say that they were just kidding. It was getting to be a "put-down free-for-all" at our family meals. I had tried talking to them about it but hadn't seen any change in their behavior.

Three things happened that helped this. One, we turned off the TV for the month of July. I was sitting down to watch TV one evening and noticed that every show we watched was oozing out of it the very things we were struggling with. Every show was very disrespectful and full of put-downs. I talked to everyone. We agreed to be TV-free for a month. You know what we found out? We had a lot more time to do things together as a family. We had really gotten in a rut as far as TV goes. It was becoming too much a part of our lives. It was an eye opener. At first it was hard to find things to do but after a few days, we were reading more, playing games together, and finding other creative things to do. Since the month is up, we haven't gotten back into watching much TV. We have watched for an evening here and there but not nearly as much as before. It was so good to get it out of our system. Now we know that there are better things to do than that.

Two, we started family devotions again, which had gone by the wayside for a while. I borrowed the book, *Family Walk* by The Navigators, from the church library. It is very simple and only takes a few minutes after supper but has made a difference already.

I know that we should never have stopped devotions in the first place because it was hard to get them going again. The enemy doesn't want us to study the Bible together as a family! We always had trouble with the kids getting serious enough to do it. Our family devotion time would end up being a time of telling them, "Sit still; be quiet; listen as I read the Bible," etc. This didn't make it something to look forward to! Now whenever we read a passage of scripture, we have them act it out together. This gives them something to do. They pay much closer attention to what is being read that way.

Three, I told the kids that any time they say something disrespectful, they will have to stand with their nose in the corner for five minutes. This was the deciding factor in curtailing it. No one wants to spend five long minutes with their nose in the corner. It makes us all more aware of our language. (I've even caught myself giving a put-down here and there!) I give them a chance to apologize before making them go to the corner, which helps them to learn the art of saying they are sorry and asking forgiveness.

These things sure make our lives as parents less hectic. Of course, we still have our struggles. Yesterday in the car on the way home from church was one of them. Everyone was so loud and boisterous! I'm thankful our God is a practical God. I trust Him to supply all our needs (for parenting) according to His riches in Christ Jesus!

Reunion!
OCTOBER 2000

"Do you know a Mary West*?" the voice on the other end of the phone was asking. (*Not her real name.)

"Yes," came Bob's reply.

The lady on the other end was notably excited, "When was the last time you saw her?"

"I probably talked to her about three weeks ago."

Bob could tell that the woman was shaken up a bit by that comment. "Only three weeks ago? You actually know her! I can't believe it! I finally found someone who's had recent contact with her!"

The story unfolded from there. The caller was Mary's sister, Betty. They had not seen each other since Betty was adopted when she was 8 and Mary was 9. Betty had been trying to find Mary for the last 9 years. She was about to give up. She had a list of phone numbers of people who lived on the street where she knew Mary had last lived. The list included us since we had only recently moved.

The problem was that Mary had moved about a year before we did and had changed her phone number several times since the listing in the phone book. Betty was so excited to finally be talking with someone who knew Mary and had talked with her recently.

We couldn't remember Mary's new number and I couldn't find where I had written it down, so I told Betty we would drive over to Mary's house and give her the information. Betty was insistent that I tell Mary to call collect if she couldn't afford to pay for the call. I think she was afraid she would not hear from her after finally finding her. We ended up talking with Betty for a half hour or so before we finally hung up to go to Mary's house. Betty hadn't wanted to let go of her first promising connection.

When Bob and I got to Mary's house, her kids told us that she had just left for work. I got her home and work phone number from them. When we got home, I called the work number and told them to have Mary call me the minute she gets in. When Mary called, it was hard to know how to break it to her. I asked her if she new a Betty Smith. I told her that Betty said she was her sister and had been trying to find her for 9 years. It sounded like the phone dropped to the floor. Mary said, "Don't hang up! Just a minute." She sat down and then kept saying, "I can't believe this! I can't believe it!"

She had to get someone to handle the customer she was working with at the time. She was crying as she took down the information, overwhelmed at what she was hearing. I found out later that she called Betty while still at work but ended up going home early and talking to her at home until 11:30 that evening!

The next day, a Sunday morning, we got a call from Mary saying that Betty was coming to see her this morning. They wanted to come over to our house after we got home from church because Betty and her husband wanted to meet us.

We spent an hour or so meeting them and hearing stories from their past. It was such a neat feeling to be a part of a reunion like this. They had not seen each other in 27 years. Mary had never been adopted. She grew up in numerous foster homes and group homes for girls. Mary has a husband in prison but recently re-dedicated her heart to Jesus, trusting Him for her provision and survival. Her husband also re-committed his life to Jesus prior to going to prison. She really needed a sister. I was so excited to see how God moved in her circumstances when she finally gave it all into His hands.

Betty was adopted by a Methodist preacher's family. She had a great life with them, but they had never let her talk about her biological family. She always felt a part of her was missing. After she left home, they finally were able to give their blessing for her to look for her lost loved ones.

Mary and Betty have since found their father, mother, all their sisters and a brother. Their mother is still hostile toward them. One brother has passed away, and there is one more brother they haven't found yet. Their father, brother, and one sister they have become reacquainted with will be coming next weekend for a family reunion with them.

It was such a privilege to be a part of this wonderful reunion. I thought about all the years we had done numerous favors for Mary. Sometimes I did the favors more out of obligation rather than an overflow of love because she was always asking for help. As I look back now, it was all worthwhile. I did it to show Jesus' love to my neighbor. I never realized I could benefit from it in this way!

You never know what a "cup of cold water in the name of Jesus" will bring. Be open to the nudging of the Holy Spirit to help others. You may end up being a part of something awesome!

EMERGENCY!
NOVEMBER 2000

"Breanna is shaking and foaming at the mouth," one of the girls from the sleepover yelled Saturday morning. It was around 11 a.m. I ran down to the basement wondering what I would see when I got to her. There she was slumped over on the couch with her eyes open yet not seeing and lots of saliva on the couch where she was laying. I started crying right away saying, "Dear Jesus!" as I headed for the phone. The other girls (8 of them) here for Breanna's 10th birthday party stood in front of her and cried, too.

"My daughter just had a seizure!" I told the 911 operator. They asked me a lot of questions to determine if she was breathing or not and said the paramedics were on their way. As I hung up the phone, I heard the sirens off in the distance coming closer to us. Breanna was already starting to "wake up." She was very groggy as she looked at me. I told her everything was okay and that the paramedics were coming. But I was weeping and acting like things were not okay. She later told me she thought someone had died when she woke up and saw all of us crying.

She kept saying she was okay. That's what she told the paramedics as they examined her, still not fully awake and still groggy. They asked if she could walk up the stairs. She said she could but stumbled as she got up so they carried her up to the waiting gurney in the kitchen.

Parents were coming to pick up their girls as the paramedics were wheeling Breanna to the ambulance. What a shock it must have been for them to see the ambulance. I answered the door and told them through tears that Breanna had a seizure and that we were going to the hospital. I asked one of them to stay with the girls until all the parents came. One of the neighborhood fathers ended up staying.

As I was leaving to ride in the ambulance, I asked one of the girls from our church to call her mom and tell her what happened. The mom started the prayer chain. She also came to the hospital and made sure I wasn't alone. I am so thankful for the comfort she offered me and the practical help she gave.

The biggest problem I faced after getting Breanna to the hospital and calming down a little was trying to get a hold of my family. One son was staying with a brother of one of the girls at the party, so he knew right away. I couldn't get through to the family Jezra was staying with. Our oldest daughter was at a soccer game and wouldn't be home until the afternoon. Bob was at a seminar in Cincinnati. He didn't have his cell phone on and neither did others from church who were with him. It wasn't until 7 p.m. that evening that I finally talked to him. I couldn't get through to his parents, either. When I did, they immediately came to the hospital and took us home after Breanna was released.

The tests they took in the emergency room all came out fine. Breanna was released after two hours. We were supposed to call our doctor on Monday and have him set up an EEG.

After we got home, Breanna slept for 2 or more hours. She was exhausted. After she woke up, she was her normal cheerful self. It was like it never happened.

When Bob got home, he talked to Breanna about what she was feeling (using the Theophostics method). She said she feared having another seizure. He told her that she should focus on that feeling. He asked Jesus to speak to Breanna. She said Jesus told her He would be with her even through another seizure. Bob asked Jesus to confirm to Breanna what He had done. She said that Jesus was singing You are my Sunshine to her. She went to her bedroom and came out with the music box she had just received last night from one of her friends. She opened it up and it played You are my Sunshine! What an awesome God we serve. Every time she plays the music box, she will be reminded of Jesus singing this song to her.

The next day after church, there was a note in our mailbox. It touched me so much I wanted to share it with you. The person who wrote it wishes to remain anonymous:

"This morning someone told me that Breanna had a seizure yesterday so I have been looking for her but couldn't find her. All morning, I have been trying to find her. When your son walked out of the service, I stopped him and asked where his little sister was. He told me she was up front with the family. I couldn't find her. I looked and looked but no Breanna. ☹

"Finally, I saw a little arm outstretched as if she was standing directly in front of her mother. Yup, there she was. I couldn't see any part of her except her right hand; it was stretched out and up praising Jesus. Then it hit me. I don't know what was going through Marla's head yesterday when Breanna was having a seizure, but I think I know what was going through her head this morning—"Breanna is here in my arms right now; I don't want to miss this moment right here. I might not have this moment (to worship God and hold Breanna at the same time) some day.

"That was a picture of God holding a new Christian, enjoying the moment to the fullest—not knowing how long this child will stay there. Also, not worried if this one child will want to go and do their own thing. (I know God is all-knowing, but I'm thinking about it in human terms.) He doesn't hold a grudge against those who choose to leave Him. Yes, I saw a picture of Christ in Marla when I saw her holding Breanna and singing. That was AWESOME!"

I had a hard time dealing with the fear that she would have another seizure. The doctor had said that she should get plenty of sleep because lack of sleep can trigger a seizure in someone who is prone to them. The very next Saturday morning, Breanna woke up feeling very tired. She said her tummy was upset and she was acting very lethargic. I was so afraid she would have another seizure. I immediately prayed, "Jesus, Breanna is Your Sunshine. I know you will take care of her. I am not going to fear anymore. I trust You with her and know that she is in Your hands." The fear left and she didn't have a seizure.

On Monday, October 30, Breanna had her EEG. I don't know the results as this newsletter goes to press. It's possible they could find nothing unusual about her brain and we may never know what caused her seizure. It's also possible they could find an abnormality in her brain, which would indicate she is seizure prone. In all the uncertainty, I know that I can trust my Heavenly Father to care for her. After all, Breanna is His Sunshine!

IT IS I, BE NOT AFRAID
DECEMBER 2000

The doctor's report from the MRI was not good. "Breanna has an abnormality in the left side of her brain. It is deep inside the brain," the doctor was saying. "We don't think it has anything to do with her seizure. But we are very concerned about this because it could be a growth or a tumor."

I was in shock. I couldn't believe that my healthy, fully-alive, 10-year-old daughter has something wrong in her brain like that. Her first seizure was on October 7, 2000. This sent us to the emergency room and began of all the tests, doctor visits, and crying out to the Lord.

The next morning, I woke up overcome with fear. I went into the living room and turned on a CD called Exodus. I wept before the Lord, telling Him that I was so scared of what was ahead of us. I couldn't seem to stop crying. I tried not to let Breanna know that I was afraid. I didn't want to put any of the fear on her. I waited until she had left for school and called a good friend. She prayed with me against the fear. She said she saw in her mind a picture of a huge 11-foot concrete wall in front of me. As she prayed, she saw a bulldozer knocking it down.

She asked the Lord to bring a scripture to mind. I immediately thought of the scripture in 2 Chronicles 20:15-18: *He said, "Listen, King Jehoshaphat and all who live in Judah and Jerusalem! This is what the LORD says to you, 'Do not be afraid or discouraged because of this vast army. For the battle is not yours, but God's. Tomorrow march down against them. They will be climbing up by the Pass of Ziz, and you will find them at the end of the gorge in the Desert of Jeruel. You will not have to fight this battle. Take up your positions; stand firm and see the deliverance the LORD will give you, O Judah and Jerusalem. Do not be afraid; do not be discouraged. Go out to face them tomorrow, and the LORD will be with you.'" Jehoshaphat bowed with his face to the ground, and all the people of Judah and Jerusalem fell down in worship before the LORD.*

The rest of the day I could stand up without fear. I know the Lord has all of this in His hands. There is nothing that surprises Him. He is sovereign and what He brings to us, He will walk through with us. Praise the Lord!

We had a visit with a neurologist in Fort Wayne. The doctor put Breanna on anti-seizure medication. The problem is that he is not sure what this "mass" is on her MRI. He told us it could be one of two things. It could be bunched up blood vessels. They probably wouldn't do anything with her right away if that was the case. They would monitor it over the years. It could be a slow-growing tumor. If this is the case, he would refer us to Riley Children's Hospital in Indianapolis. He wanted to have a respected radiologist look at the MRI films and see if he could tell what it was.

The next day I got a call from the doctor. The radiologist couldn't tell either. They will call a neurosurgeon at the Children's Hospital and set up an appointment for Breanna. We are on to more testing and more doctors. Will this ever end?

Another thing that I was concerned about was how our children were dealing with this. Last night after supper we asked each one how they were feeling about the stuff Breanna was going through. Everyone, including Breanna, said they felt peace. Praise the Lord! We have a wonderful Father who cares for His own.

God is in control. He is our shepherd. We have no needs. He makes us lie down in green pastures. He guides us in paths of righteousness for His name's sake. He leads us by peaceful streams. He restores our soul. We can walk through the valley of the shadow of death and fear no evil because His rod and His staff, they comfort us! He prepares a table before us in the presence of our enemies. He anoints our head with oil. Surely goodness and mercy will follow us all the days of our lives and we will dwell in the house of the Lord forever! (Psalm 23 paraphrased by me.)

When Jesus walked across the water, the disciples were very afraid. Jesus said to them, "It is I, be not afraid." Jesus is saying that to us. "It is I, be not afraid. I am in charge of the storms in your life and I will calm them in my time and in my way. You can trust me!" Praise His name!

PRAYERS FOR BREANNA
DECEMBER 2000 (CONT.)
WRITTEN WHILE ON A TRIP

It has been three months since Breanna's seizure that led to us finding out she had a brain tumor. We made a trip to Florida with my extended family over Thanksgiving. My aunt lives near where we were staying. She had moved here a few years ago to retire in a warmer climate. While we were there, she showed me a prayer list with Breanna's name on it. It said, "Pray for Breanna Brenneman – brain tumor, second MRI."

"We are going to see the answer to that prayer," I said, as tears formed in my eyes. My family comforted me as I cried. I want so much for this prayer to be answered. If it isn't, we have a lot to face. To know a group of senior citizens I have never met are praying for my daughter is overwhelming. I had put all of this health issue behind me to enjoy the trip with my family, but those written words brought it all to the surface again.

We are facing a mountain but Jesus moves mountains. Jesus said in Matthew 17:20, *"I tell you the truth, if you have faith as small as a mustard seed, you can say to this mountain, 'Move from here to there' and it will move. Nothing will be impossible for you."*

Even though Breanna has a tumor, I believe that God is going to move it in His timing and in His way. I choose to believe that nothing is impossible for God.

Are you going through a tough time right now? Put your little faith in the hands of a big God and watch as He moves mountains out of your path. I trust Him to do this for Breanna. I trust Him to do it for you, too.

Reflections
WHILE SEARCHING

GOD'S WAITING ROOM

I feel like I have been in and out of God's waiting room for three months now, since Breanna had a seizure. We have had tests and have waited for the results. We have had doctor visits where we were referred to specialists so had to wait for those appointments to come. Last month we got the results from the neurosurgeon. The doctor's report couldn't be worse! The tumor in Breanna's brain is in a dangerous place—on the brain stem. Even though it is the size of a pea, it is both dangerous to let it go and dangerous to do anything about it. Even though it is awful news, it was good to finally have the answers to what was in Breanna's brain. The neurosurgeon at the Children's Hospital, had no question what the MRI showed.

This sent us into God's waiting room again with the hope of God shrinking her tumor before the next MRI. There are some physical signs that show this might be already beginning to happen—Breanna's droopy smile seems to be less pronounced than it once was. Yet we know that the next MRI, scheduled this month, will confirm or deny this. No matter what, we know that God is sovereign and in control of what is happening to our child.

The word "wait" is mentioned 92 times in the Bible. A lot of those times are from Old Testament stories about someone lying in wait for someone else and other similar uses, but I found that most of the ones in the Psalms are about waiting for the Lord—being in God's waiting room. Here are a few of my favorites:

Psalm 5:3 *In the morning, O Lord, you hear my voice; in the morning I lay my requests before you and wait in expectation.*

Psalm 33:20 *We wait in hope for the Lord; He is our help and our shield.*

Psalm 37:7 *Be still before the Lord and wait patiently for Him.*

Psalm 37:34 *Wait for the Lord and keep His way. He will exalt you to inherit the land; when the wicked are cut off, you will see it.*

Psalm 38:15 *I wait for you, O Lord; you will answer, O Lord my God.*

Psalm 130:5-6 *I wait for the Lord, my soul waits, and in His word I put my hope. My soul waits for the Lord more than watchmen wait for the morning.*

Praise the Lord! His waiting room is for those who wait expectantly! We are waiting expectantly for Him to give us an answer. He is our help and our shield. Waiting for Him is waiting with expectation that He will do what He has promised. We can trust Him with our daughter, knowing His timing and His deliverance is coming! We will inherit the land! We can wait because the Lord is just and true and the purposes He has for Breanna will be accomplished!

SITTING AT THE FEET OF JESUS

FEBRUARY 2001

Luke 10:38-42 gives the account of Jesus at the home of Mary and Martha. In verse 41 Jesus says, *"Martha, Martha, you are worried and upset by so many things, but only one thing is needed. Mary has chosen what is better, and it will not be taken away from her."*

I am a vintage Martha. When a task is at hand, I have a hard time concentrating on anything else. I get up in the morning determined to spend quality time with the Lord. But by the time my feet hit the floor, I start seeing all the things that need to be done. I have such a hard time letting it go and concentrating on the Lord. I'm also guilty of making the time with the Lord just another task and going through the motions without really being there. *Oops, I need ten minutes of journaling, ten minutes of worship, and oh, I didn't read four chapters of scripture today.* That's the way my thoughts will go if I let them.

During a recent personal ministry time, I heard the Lord say to me (I'm paraphrasing), "Marla, Marla, don't you know that I don't want to be another thing on your agenda? I don't want you to do things when we are together. I want you to be in my presence. Sit at my feet and spend time with me without your agenda. I want to spend time with you, not just be something you check off your to-do list. Lay it all down and sit at my feet and enjoy my presence."

I'm not saying that reading the Bible, worshipping, and journaling isn't important. But when it gets to the place of being a rote exercises, then it isn't a relationship with Jesus, it's just another thing on the list.

I choose to spend time soaking in God's presence in silence before Him, listening to His heartbeat and following what He wants from me. This is the best time of fellowship with the Master. I can do all kinds of things for Him, but if I haven't gotten the instructions from the Master Himself, it is just busywork. *"Marla, Marla, you are worried and upset about many things but only one thing is needed. Mary has chosen what is better and it will not be taken from her."*

I want what is better, don't you? I used to feel like Jesus was being so hard on Martha. After all, she was preparing a meal for her Master, taking care of everyday needs. This isn't bad. But I realize that I can get so busy with serving the Master that I have no time to spend at His feet. It's not wrong to do my routine tasks but it is good to remain open to the times of visitation when Jesus wants me to spend time at His feet, soaking in His presence, so I will be prepared for what His agenda is for me.

"Jesus, I'm ready. Let me sit at Your feet for the next half hour or so and enjoy You and You speak to me Your agenda for the day! Let me hear from You, the One thing that is needed for this hour!"

MY CHURCH EXPERIENCES
MARCH 2001

My church background growing up was unique. My parents come from a very conservative church, which they left when I was about 2 years old. I don't have any memory of us going there as a child.

Soon after, my parents helped start a neighborhood church with a few other families. My memories of church life start in this small family church. My dad helped pastor there. We did a lot of things together with the other families. I remember feeling a deep sense of God's presence during the services. I was around 8 when we left this congregation. I later found out it was because my parents had received the Holy Spirit and the others didn't approve.

My dad had heard of a group that was meeting in a bordering state. We ended up traveling 3½ hours every Sunday morning to go to church. I think my mom and dad felt they had found THE church—God's chosen people. This church was not supposed to have "rules." We were all supposed to follow the Lord. But there were a lot of "unspoken" rules. For example, the women wore plain head coverings and floor-length dresses with a cape. Eventually every woman dressed like that so they would not look less "spiritual."

Many strange teachings were gradually introduced and accepted. One major teaching was about "Angel Ministry." The leader of our group received this ministry, which made him one step above everyone else. He would hear from God for all of us. We could not question what he told us because it was straight from God. There was a lot of what Bill Hamon calls "spooky spiritual" going on. This man would be slain in the spirit during a church service. While he lay there like a dead man (that's what it looked like to me as a child) he would receive prophetic words from the Lord. When he would "wake up" a new teaching was introduced that no one could question. A lot of very unhealthy rules were "adopted" this way. A controlling spirit was at work in a big way. Many marriages and families were destroyed and people were hurt deeply.

I remember sitting in church singing a hymn and making an error like putting the word "I" or "me" in the place of the word "God" so it would sound like I was praising myself. An inner voice would tell me that I really meant to do that because I didn't believe in God. I saw all kinds of manifestations of the spirit around me, but I didn't ever feel any of it. That confirmed to me that God couldn't use me. I was too bad. I would hear condemning words in my mind saying I would never measure up. I would never be "spiritual" enough. I saw God as very stern and demanding. If I didn't follow every letter of the law, I would never make it. I often felt that the ten or twelve ministers who sat up front facing the congregation were looking directly at me with condemnation. I really didn't want anything to do with a God like that but felt compelled to try and obey because the consequences of not obeying were too great: eternity in hell!

After we stopped going to this church, I found a traditional congregation to attend where there was absolutely nothing charismatic about it. It felt safe. I met Bob in this congregation. After a few years though, I became filled with the Holy Spirit and wasn't satisfied in a church that didn't believe in the gifts of the Spirit.

When we came to this church, I was still very scared of any manifestations of the Spirit. I felt I had to be "super spiritual" to be used by God. It was here that I began to heal. It was a process of life-changing experiences of coming face to face with the love that Jesus has for me. It was hard but I finally accepted that love. I now know that He would have died for me if I was the only one in this world. What love! I've received teaching on how to hear God's voice and I actually hear Him speak to me! I began to let go and speak in tongues which I never was able to do before. I am still very timid about it when others can hear me but it has been a gift that has built me up in my spirit. I had seen such abuse of these spiritual gifts. It is refreshing to see them used the way God intended.

There is a balance here at this church that is freeing. There is an openness to the Spirit's leading, but the focus is not on the manifestations. The focus is on life-change. God moves in so many different ways. I've known people who would go here, there, and everywhere just to have an experience with the Lord, yet their lives were a wreck. What difference did the experience have in bringing life-change? God's purpose in bringing any of the manifestations of His Spirit is to change us. 1 Corinthians 12:7 says, *Now to each one the manifestation of the Spirit is given for the common good.* What I witnessed as a child was not the kind of change that brings life! It only brought death and destruction. Jesus came to bring life. I'm glad I've found that life in Jesus Christ through being a part of a healthy church community.

THE PRAYER OF JABEZ
APRIL 2001

The Prayer of Jabez by Bruce Wilkinson is a little book that will have a BIG impact on your life. Bob and I first heard about this little book when we were at Teaching the Word Ministries in Leola, Pennsylvania for a seminar. A lot of the people at the seminar were talking about the prayer of Jabez. They tried to explain it to us but without having read the book, it was hard to totally understand what they were talking about. I made a mental note to get the book for myself.

When we returned home, I put it on the back burner and didn't think about it for a long time. Then while working in the church office, I came across a catalog with this book featured. I showed it to the church librarian and asked if she would consider purchasing it for the church library. She did. It came to the church along with a lot of other library items. I took the book, started skimming through it, and was very intrigued by what I was reading. I was tempted to take it home and read it before it was processed into the library, but decided to wait

After a week had gone by, I noticed that other material from that package was in the library but not The Prayer of Jabez. I asked the librarian where it was. She told me that she'd had it at home ready to put the card in the back. But when she got around to working on it she discovered that her husband had read it and had highlighted things in it that stood out to him. (This shows what an intriguing book it is!) She had to purchase another one for the library and that's why it was taking so long.

When I got to church the next morning, she had laid the book on my desk already checked out for me to take home.

Since then, other people have purchased copies for themselves after hearing about it. (They didn't want to wait until I got finished with it, I guess!) I read it to our kids during devotional time after supper. We are praying the prayer as a family now. I also purchased my own copy of it. God wants to do something awesome in the lives of people who are willing to open themselves up to His blessing and influence.

The book is about a man named Jabez listed in 1 Chronicles chapter 4 in the middle of a list of genealogy names. There are two verses—1 Chron. 4:9-10—dedicated to Jabez and then it goes back to listing names. It says that Jabez was more honorable than his brothers. The prayer that he prayed is in verse 10. At the end of the verse it says that God granted his request. This prayer is a prayer that God loves to answer. The book shows the parts of the prayer and how they can be used in our own lives. It also has a lot of examples of what God is doing in the lives of people who are praying the prayer.

I recommend reading this book with an open mind to what God can do through a prayer that he enjoys answering. You never know what can happen when you ask God to bless you indeed and enlarge your territory!

A LETTER TO MY DAUGHTER, AMBER

JUNE 2001

Where has the time gone? It was just yesterday that we found out we were going to have you, our first child. I was so happy! To be a mom was my highest calling. I had dreamed of this day since I was a little girl.

At first you seemed like just an extension of me, not a separate person at all. Then, as you grew, you became more and more independent of me. You were your own person with your own ideas and feelings. Those early days were spent trying to be the best mother I could be. I worried about every little thing. I thought that each mistake I made would damage you for life. Everything was so serious. What if you rebelled or turned your back on God when you got older? What if you were wounded by the words I said? What if I wasn't really cut out to be a parent?

Now as I look back over 18 years of parenting, I see things from a different perspective. It wasn't so much about what kind of parent I was, it was about serving a great God who listens to the heart cries of a mother on her knees as she asks for forgiveness for the harsh words she had spoken or cries out to God for the behavior of her child! When He became the center of your life, being a parent was easy! You have become a wonderful young woman. I enjoy seeing you grow in the Lord.

I remember a time while homeschooling that I corrected your math paper and you got all the problems right. I was shocked because you always had 2 or 3 errors. I didn't think too much about it, though. A week later, you burst out crying and confessed to having cheated on that paper by looking at the answers in the teacher's manual. It was a revelation to me to see how God was working in your life even when I wasn't aware of the problem.

You have been a great friend. I enjoy the times we spend talking and laughing together after the younger kids are in bed. There are times when we cry and pray together about what is happening in our lives. Remember the poem I wrote you? I tried to put into words all that you meant to me. It was from my heart even though it sounds so corny now.

You blessed me so many times with your faith and trust in God. We cried together when we found out about Breanna's tumor. You were so strong through all of the uncertainty. Because you had taken anatomy, you were able to answer some of the questions I had forgotten to ask the doctor. Your strong faith keeps me strong, too, as we go through this process. You watched as I had my bout with cancer ten years ago. I think God gave you a special faith and trust in Him during that time which is helping you be strong during this trial.

What does the future hold? We will continue our relationship long distance when God leads you to India as a missionary, something you have known would happen since you were a child. I see some doors opening with relationships at the University that will move you closer to that goal. I know that it will be difficult to be so far away. I also know that God will give us strength to make it through.

My prayer for you is that you will follow the leading of the Holy Spirit no matter where He leads. I pray that I will be able to accept wherever God leads you (even to India as a long-term missionary if that is His will). I pray that you will grow in your relationship with God. May you continue to be a light to your generation.

I thank God for the privilege of being your mom. You are a gift that keeps on giving. I love you!

Reflections
DURING STRUGGLES

Downward Spiral

Last night I had a crisis. I could feel myself being pulled into another emotional breakdown. I sensed a spiritual attack but felt powerless to combat it. It was a real battle for me. I have had two major emotional breakdowns in my life. I felt as if I was never going to be strong again. Bob listened as I talked and cried through all my fears. The most prevalent fear was what others would think if they knew that I wasn't a strong person. I felt like I battled all night long even in my dreams.

This morning, I sensed the Lord tell me to read my journal. Earlier this month when we were on a trip, I had written a word that the Lord had given to me. As I read it, I knew it spoke to the struggle that I had just gone through the night before.

This is what I had sensed the Lord saying almost three weeks before: "*My daughter, wake up and be alert. The enemy wants to pull you into his trap. Don't take the bait. Stand up and stay alert. I am leading you but you haven't been listening. Begin doing the things I'm asking you to do and you will see the doors open. Begin being obedient. Begin writing again. Walk in the truth you know. Other people need to hear what I've done in your life. This may put you in a very vulnerable position, but I am calling you to bless others by speaking out about where you've been and what I've done in your life. Show people your struggles so they know you are human and have difficulties; that you don't have it all together. You were created to write and you feel like you aren't going anywhere because you aren't writing. Walk into what I have for you and you will begin to see My glory and My will for you. Walk on, dear daughter. Don't stay where you are!*"

(For a year, as you can see, I hadn't written the church newsletter column. I had started working in the church office and began feeling uncomfortable being so vulnerable. I also knew I wasn't as close to God as I had been. I was choosing to go through the motions, instead of being engaged in my relationship with Jesus. This word really jolted me out of my complacency.)

I can't put it off any longer. I must begin to be obedient to the Father. I know that it is the root of the attack that I felt last night. Would I be obedient and open my life up to others or would I continue to hide behind the masks I had put on to make it seem that I had it all together? I choose to follow the Lord. I pray that you are blessed by my obedience.

COMFORT IN TIMES OF TROUBLE
SEPTEMBER 2002

I wrote the article last month in this newsletter thinking that I was over the "emotional breakdown." The next evening after the newsletter was in the church mailboxes, I was at the deepest pit of anxiety and despair I had ever been in. I never dreamed that when I wrote that article, it would become more real to me. I thought it was over. I thought I wouldn't have to be any more vulnerable than that, but God had other ideas. Through this very deep struggle, I have had another level of healing that would have never come had I not gone through what I did.

I have learned that I don't need to be a "strong person." My strength is in God. I learned that we need to be open and honest with others about our struggles because there are other people struggling the same way, thinking they are the only ones going through it. When God brings us through something, He wants us to tell others so we can be an encouragement to them. 2 Corinthians 1:4-5 tells us, ...*who comforts us in all our troubles, so that we can comfort those in any trouble with the comfort we ourselves have received from God. For just as the sufferings of Christ flow over into our lives, so also through Christ our comfort overflows.* This is what God wants to do with all of us. If we don't share what God is doing in our lives, we miss blessing others.

One night during the worst of the "crisis," I woke up at 1 a.m. in the middle of a panic attack. I had been dreaming. When I woke up I didn't know what was real and what wasn't. A huge wave of worry swept over me with the fear attached that said I wasn't healed at all. These two old hymn choruses kept going through my mind:

Peace, peace, wonderful peace
Coming down from the Father above
Sweep over my spirit forever, I pray,
In fathomless billows of love.

We have an anchor that keeps the soul
Steadfast and sure while the billows roll
Fastened to the Rock which cannot move
Grounded firm and deep in the Saviour's love

When the circumstances around me were so "stormy" and the "billows" of panic and anxiety were overwhelming me, I clung to the truth of these choruses like someone drowning clings to a life raft. They helped me to press through the attack and find peace even when the "billows of fear" were rushing over me. Those "fathomless billows of love" were stronger than the hugest "billows of fear!"

You, too, can find that peace during the storms that want to overtake you. God is so faithful! He can be trusted to sustain us through the deepest and darkest trial we are going through. Cling to Him who loves you so much He was willing to go through the most horrendous pain so that He could have a relationship with you for eternity!

FIGHTING HOPELESSNESS
OCTOBER 2002

Romans 15:13 says, "*May the God of hope fill you with all joy and peace as you trust in Him, so that you may overflow with hope by the power of the Holy Spirit.*"

Each of us goes through times where we think that there is no hope. I have often felt like it's hopeless when I go through an emotional struggle. Thoughts like *I am not going to make it through this* or *it will never get any better* go through my mind.

These kinds of thoughts are not from God. Anytime we have thoughts like this, we are agreeing with the enemy about our situation. The problem is that sometimes we have a very hard time fighting these thoughts.

II Corinthians 10:5 talks about taking every thought captive and making it obedient to Christ. When I get a thought that I know is not from God, I take it captive by saying out loud something like this: "I am not going to believe this lie! I submit to God's word that says I have hope by the power of the Holy Spirit."

I say it out loud so the enemy can hear me. It also helps for me to hear it, too. I fight these thoughts by consciously choosing not to believe them and choosing to believe the Word of God.

Sometimes it is very hard for me to do this on my own. I have called friends and asked them to pray with me when I couldn't seem to do it myself. Having someone else agree with me and pray with me strengthens me and helps me to fight the battle.

God wants to teach us how to be strong and be able to stand against the devil's schemes. We do this by fighting the enemy and his tactics to bring us down. Each battle we win helps us to have more strength for the next one that comes.

Friends, if you are in a situation that seems hopeless, don't give up or give in to the enemy. Trust in the Lord and be filled with all joy and peace so that you may overflow with hope by the power of the Holy Spirit.

LIVING A THANKFUL LIFE
NOVEMBER 2002

The Bible says in 1 Thessalonians 5:18, "...*give thanks in all circumstances for this is God's will for you in Christ Jesus.*"

Thankfulness can change attitudes very quickly. This week, our family was in a very bad mood. Actually, if the truth be known, I was the one with the bad attitude. I couldn't seem to shake it. I had a run in with one of the kids and I didn't feel good about the way I handled it. I was still very upset by it all. You've all heard the phrase, "When Mom's not happy, ain't nobody happy." Well, it seemed to be true that evening!

At the dinner table that evening, I asked everyone to say one thing they were thankful for. Right away, the mood began to change.

After we had finished that, I asked everyone to say one good thing about each family member. We began with our oldest son. Everyone said one thing about him that they admired. One rule we established was that it couldn't be a put-down in disguise like, "One thing I like about him is that he isn't as good looking as I am." (One person actually tried to say something like that!)

We had a lot of fun. We were all laughing heartily when we finished. The whole mood around the table had improved.

I was surprised by what the kids came up with for each other. They are very perceptive about who their siblings really are. It was so neat to watch what happened. When we began seeing the good in each other, the negative attitude couldn't live there anymore.

It is good practice to be thankful. It's hard to be in a bad mood when we begin to look at all God has done for us.

I would encourage you to do an exercise like this at your family table. Or try it around your extended family table at Thanksgiving. There is nothing like bringing out the good in each other and bringing glory to God in the process.

According to the Veggie Tale video, *Madam Blueberry*, a thankful heart is a happy heart. So let's sow happiness wherever we go.

Reflections
OF ENCOURAGEMENT

Training For Godliness This New Year

JANUARY 2003

Every year it's the same old thing: those awful New Year's resolutions. I make a long list of things I'm determined to change about my life. I resolve to get up earlier so I can spend more time with the Lord. I resolve to be nicer to the kids. I resolve to eat healthier and exercise more.

It usually lasts about a day or two and then something happens and the list is history.

Why can't I do it? It's not for lack of trying. I've tried and tried. It's not for lack of determination. I'm determined to change for the better. It's not because I don't want to do the things on my list. The problem lies in the fact that there is an immense difference between training to do something and trying to do something. I learned this from reading a book by John Ortberg called, *The Life You've Always Wanted.* He gave the word picture of someone being asked to run a marathon. They had never run before in their life. Do you think they could go out and win the marathon? No! They could try all they wanted to run the marathon but would never make it. If they began a training program of running a little more each day, then they would eventually be able to make it.

Spiritual transformation is the same way. It's not a matter of trying harder but of training wisely. Paul says to Timothy, "…train yourself for godliness."

Ortberg says, "Following Jesus simply means learning from Him how to arrange my life around activities that enable me to live in the fruit of the Spirit."

Doesn't that sound a lot better than resolving to do better and failing over and over again? Training for godliness means establishing habits or spiritual disciplines that help me as I train to become more like Christ.

This year my resolution is to become more like Jesus by training for godliness. That sounds like a tangible goal, doesn't it? I think I will make it! If I mess up, I'll just pick myself back up and do it again. What freedom this is from the "trying and failing" routine!

DOWN IN THE DUMPS
MARCH 2003

I struggle during the winter months with feeling down and depressed. Things look bleaker to me during these months. I don't have much enthusiasm for anything. It's hard to get excited about doing something new. I struggle finding hope that things will get any better.

I struggle with my quiet time with the Lord. I don't really feel like being in His presence. All I want to do is sit down and watch TV. I guess watching TV and movies becomes a kind of escape from my dull, dreary life.

This year hasn't been as bad as other years, but I still struggle. I feel like a cloud is hanging over me that I can't get past. With all the days of no sun, it gets worse and worse.

I know many people struggle this same way during the winter months. There is hope for us. I know in my heart and mind that I don't need to give in to these feelings. I know if I act on how I feel, I will only feel worse. If I continue to escape by watching TV and movies, I will still feel the same—maybe even worse—after the show is over.

I know that stepping out and doing what God tells me no matter how I feel will bring me out of it. A step of obedience—like putting on a worship CD and praising the Lord even when I don't feel like it—brings me to the place of feeling different. It brings Light into the darkness of my despair.

This is what James 1:2-8 says in The Message, "*Consider it a sheer gift, friends, when tests and challenges come at you from all sides. You know that under pressure, your faith-life is forced into the open and shows its true colors. So don't try to get out of anything prematurely. Let it do its work so you become mature and well developed, not deficient in any way.*

"*If you don't know what you're doing, pray to the Father. He loves to help. You'll get His help, and won't be condescended to when you ask for it. Ask boldly, believingly, without a second thought. People who 'worry their prayers' are like wind-whipped waves. Don't think you're going to get anything from the Master that way; adrift at sea, keeping all your options open.*"

When I give in to the feelings, I am being tossed about, wind-whipped, and adrift at sea. My problem is that I haven't asked God who gives generously. I haven't taken the step of obedience and walked through the test and challenge. These tests are there to bring me to maturity so that I won't be deficient in any way. Instead, I have tried to avoid the tests and challenges, which results in becoming tossed and whipped by the wind.

I'm glad that God loves to help us when we ask Him. Maybe next time I begin to feel down, I will remember that I don't have to give in to the feelings. I can ask God to help and continue to do what He's called me to do in spite of how I feel.

Jesus, I pray that each one who is experiencing feelings of depression and despair will be strong enough to not give in to them but to ask You for help. You won't be condescending in any way to them. You will open Your arms to them and give them what they ask for. I pray for boldness in asking for help from You, Jesus. I pray for boldness in stepping out in obedience to Your Word. Amen.

(I am talking here about mild feelings of despair, not anxiety disorder, panic attacks, or clinical depression. Please seek professional help or some kind of freedom ministry if you can't cope with everyday life and are having thoughts of suicide or of hurting yourself or others. I've been there, too, and received help from going through freedom ministry and also getting on medication. –Marla)

LIVING LIKE AN HEIR TO THE THRONE
APRIL 2003

Have you seen the movie, *Princess Diaries*? It's about an ordinary girl who lives in San Francisco with her mother. Her parents divorced when she was a baby and her father had recently died. She finds out that she is heir to the throne of Genovia, a small country her father's family is from.

Her grandmother comes and tries to convince her to take her place as princess. She agrees to have her grandmother work with her and help her walk and talk like royalty. The task isn't easy. She is very clumsy and knows nothing of princess etiquette. It takes a while to get the old nature out of her and to get her to carry herself as a princess.

The girl isn't sure she really wants to be a princess. But she does begin to enjoy the attention of a very popular boy in her class on whom she'd had a crush for a long time. She finds out that this guy isn't all she had dreamed he would be. She eventually realizes he isn't really interested in her, only her fame and beauty.

She wrestles with the decision to become the princess with all the demands and expectations the title holds. In the end she understands that with the title comes an opportunity to help people that living her ordinary life wouldn't bring. She realizes her life can be used for the greater good, not just for her own selfish desires. She has a destiny!

We are all like this girl. We begin our walk very clumsily and selfishly—not realizing the destiny our King has for us.

As we begin to walk and act like the heirs we are, we realize our lives are more than just about our own selfish desires. It's not just what we want but what our King wants for us that matters.

We wrestle with our flesh all the time. We try to live in the Spirit but have trouble putting to death the old nature. We must win the battle against our fleshly desires. We must begin to live like sons and daughters of the King. We must not let satan deceive us into believing that we are illegitimate children without a destiny.

It's like we are living in a foreign land, not realizing that we belong in the Kingdom of our King where we have all the blessing of our Father, the King, at our disposal. Wake up and realize the destiny God has for you. Don't live like paupers any longer!

Ephesians 4:17-24 in *THE MESSAGE* says, *"And so I insist—and God backs me up on this—that there be no going along with the crowd, the empty-headed, mindless crowd. They've refused for so long to deal with God that they've lost touch not only with God but with reality itself. They can't think straight anymore. Feeling no pain, they let themselves go in sexual obsession, addicted to every sort of perversion.*

"But that's no life for you. You learned Christ! My assumption is that you have paid careful attention to him, been well instructed in the truth precisely as we have it in Jesus. Since, then, we do not have the excuse of ignorance, everything—and I do mean everything—connected with that old way of life has to go. It's rotten through and through. Get rid of it! And then take on an entirely new way of life—a God-fashioned life, a life renewed from the inside and working itself into your conduct as God accurately reproduces his character in you."

Which way do you want to live, the life of the mindless, empty-headed crowd or the life of the Spirit which reproduces God's character? I choose to live a God-fashioned life, a life renewed from the inside and working itself into my conduct as God accurately reproduces His character in me. I'm not there yet, but I'm on my way, as God continues His work of helping me become the princess I'm destined to be.

A NEW LOOK AT THE 23RD PSALM

MAY 2003

I am reading a book called, *Traveling Light* by Max Lucado. It is a unique perspective of the 23rd Psalm that gives help for the burdens we carry in our everyday life.

The author tells us that we are carrying way too much luggage around with us in our daily lives that we were never meant to bear. Do any of you carry around fear? Anxiety? Discontent? Hopelessness? Guilt? Worry? Grief? Shame? Loneliness? The list goes on and on.

Can you picture our Shepherd leading us to quiet waters and helping us to "walk through the valley of the shadow of death?" He wants us to let Him carry the burdens so that we have the energy to carry the load we were designed for.

In the chapter on fear, the author begins with the passage of scripture in Luke 22:39-44 where Jesus is praying before His crucifixion asking the Father, *"If You are willing, take away this cup of suffering. But do what You want, not what I want"* (NCV). He talks about the pain in Jesus' face and the sweat like drops of blood falling to the ground.

We don't often think about how Jesus must have looked at that moment. He was in anguish. He was very fearful of what He would face. He was so afraid that He bled. Severe anxiety can cause a breakdown of the capillaries in the sweat glands. When this occurs, sweat comes out tinged with blood.

When Jesus was at this point, the first place He went was to His Heavenly Father. David did the same thing. He said in Psalm 23:4, "I will fear no evil." He knew where to look: "You are with me. Your rod and staff they comfort me."

Jesus doesn't think our fears are foolish or silly. He won't tell you to "buck up" or "get tough." He's been there where you are. He knows how you feel (*Traveling Light* p. 101).

Philippians 4:6 says, *"Don't be anxious about anything but in everything, with prayer and petition, with thanksgiving, present your requests to God.*" When we are in an anxious situation, don't measure the size of the mountain, talk to the One who can move it.

It's up to you. You can carry the burdens that you weren't meant to bear. Or you can give them to the One who wants to carry them. Let Him walk with you through your struggles and trials. Don't try to go it alone!

I hope this whets your appetite for this wonderful book. It has been a real help to me and to my oldest daughter.

No Longer A Teenager

June 2003

Amber just celebrated her 20th birthday on Wednesday. She is no longer a teenager. The changes in our relationship over the last two years have been hard for me and yet it is exciting to step into a new way of relating as one adult to another.

I have had to let go of being involved in her everyday life. I have had to trust God to take care of her. I have had to let go of giving her unsolicited advice. I'm still her mom and always will be but the relationship has had to change. This wasn't an "all of the sudden" letting go. It began the minute she was born. Every milestone in her life became a step in the letting go process. It was very hard to do but it had to be done to help her become a responsible adult.

The biggest change was when she went off to college. For the first time in her life, she lived away from home for more than a couple weeks at a time. I didn't know what she was doing all the time. I didn't have any control over what she ate, how much sleep she got, or who she was with. I had to trust that she would make wise choices without me being involved.

Now, she is away for the summer and I've had to let go a little more. She is on her own and may never live under my roof again. Facing that fact has been hard. It means that our relationship will never be what it once was. I have to accept this and begin to walk out the new role of being the mom to an adult on her own.

Of course I will always be her mother. We find ways to connect and talk with each other even when she lives miles apart. If I hadn't let go and was trying to hang on, our relationship would be strained. As it is, I have a wonderful friendship with her. I am very thankful for it. I treasure the fact that she wants to talk to me about what is going on in her life.

I have been a parent for twenty years now. I know that I didn't do everything right. I have made many mistakes (and am still making them!) along the way. I am thankful for the way God is working in each of our children in spite of my parenting errors and blunders!

I agree with John when he said in 3 John 1:4, "*I have no greater joy than to hear that my children are walking in the truth.*" I know he was talking about his spiritual children in this verse but it is such a joy as a parent to see our children walking with the Lord; to see each of them develop a personal relationship with Jesus that will last through eternity and sustain them when the difficulties come. Thank you, Jesus, for being faithful to me and my family!

YOU ARE PRECIOUS TO GOD!

JULY 2003

Last night I heard a couple women share about adoption from the perspective of being the adopted child. Some other women shared from the perspective of a parent adopting children. I was so moved by the need for the kids being adopted to feel like they belong. Both of the adopted ladies have struggled with feeling out of place and unwanted even though they lived in wonderful adoptive families.

One lady shared about her foster and adopted kids not always being able to receive the love she and her husband have for them.

How much more does our Father in heaven want us to receive the love He has for us that made Him willing to send His only Son to die for our sins? While we each were dirty with sin-stains, He looked past the filth and saw a precious child of God who has value and worth.

Even though one of the adopted ladies knew the verse in Psalm 139 about being *"fearfully and wonderfully made"* she didn't believe it applied to her because she was conceived by an unwed teenage mother. How could God form her in the womb when she was born because of sin? It took her until adulthood to realize that she wasn't a mistake and that she belonged to God because He created her to be who she was and placed her in a family.

My prayer is that each of us will be able to grasp *"how wide and long and high and deep is the love of Christ"* (Ephesians 3:18). It doesn't matter what the circumstances of our birth are. We are fearfully and wonderfully made. God formed us in our mother's womb to be the person He designed us to be. There are no exceptions to this truth! May this realization go from our heads into our hearts!

NEW WAY OF STUDYING THE BIBLE

AUGUST 2003

I began a new way to do my quiet time with the Lord last week. It has helped me to have a more meaningful time with Him. Rick Warren's book, *Personal Bible Study Methods*, really helped me with this. It has an appendix in the back called, "Developing a meaningful quiet time." This method has really rejuvenated my spiritual life. It brought an excitement for my time with the Lord that I haven't had in a long time. Let me show you how Rick Warren suggests doing a meaningful quiet time.

The first thing you have to have is a good attitude. You should come with expectancy, reverence, alertness, and willingness to obey.

You should have a specific time when you are at your best.

You need to find a place to study that isn't too comfortable that you fall asleep but isn't uncomfortable so you want to get done quickly. It should be a place where there are few distractions and where you can pray aloud without disturbing others. It should have good lighting. I found a desk in Bob's office to be the best place for me.

You will need a Bible, a notebook, a hymnbook, or CD to play. The first thing to do is relax and focus on God and wait on Him. I begin by asking the Lord to clear my mind of distractions and help me to focus on Him. If a task comes to mind that distracts me, I write it down to do later. Pray briefly asking the Lord to illuminate the scripture you are going to read for the day. Read a portion of scripture—not a study of the Bible, only a short passage. Read it slowly, repeatedly, without stopping, aloud, and systematically to get a sweep of the passage.

Meditate on what the passage is saying. You can put the passage in your own words. You can make it personal by inserting your name in the passage as you read it. You can ask questions using the SPACE PETS acrostic:

Is there any:
    S-sin to confess?
    P-promise to claim?
    A-attitude to adjust?
    C-command to obey?
    E-example to follow?
    P-prayer to pray?
    E-error to avoid?
    T-truth to believe?
    S-something to praise God for?

Write down what God shows you during this meditation time.

Next you should apply the scripture to your life by making a statement of what you will do that is practical, possible, and provable. Write this down in your notebook.

Find a verse in your reading that you want to "chew" on all day and memorize it. Or begin a Bible memory program of some kind.

Now is your time of prayer. Use the acrostic PRAY:

P-praise the Lord (read a Psalm of praise, sing a song to the Lord,
    or play a worship CD.
R-repent of your sins.
A-ask for yourself and others (intercession).
Y-yield yourself to God's will for the day.

Rick Warren suggests varying your plan so you don't fall into a rut or the trap of performing instead of getting to know Christ. His ideas for variation are to spend a whole quiet time in thanksgiving or spend the whole time in scripture memory.

Before I began using this method, I had a hard time incorporating scripture into my quiet time. I would read a passage but not actually work at applying it to my life. This has been so helpful in allowing God to speak to me through the scriptures. It has also been a lot of fun.

The first three days I read three different passages and each one dealt with fear.

The first one was Psalm 15. I chose the first and last part of the chapter to memorize: "*He whose walk is blameless and who does what is righteous ... will never be shaken.*" I have suffered from anxiety attacks that have really shaken me up. I claimed this promise. I confessed to the Lord ways in which I have not walked blamelessly or done what was righteous. I committed to doing what is righteous in the future.

The second day it was Psalm 34. I memorized verse 4, "*I sought the Lord and He answered me; He delivered me from ALL my fears.*" I confessed aloud that I choose to seek Jesus and allow Him to deliver me from ALL my fears, not just some of them.

The third day I read 1 John 4. The verse that I chose to memorize was verse 18, "*There is no fear in love. But perfect love drives out fear, because fear has to do with punishment. The one who fears is not made perfect in love.*"

I choose to stand on this promise of abiding in Jesus' perfect love that will drive out fear.

It was amazing to me that the first three days of scripture reading were about fear. God wanted me to know that He was able to deliver me from all my fears. I didn't need to be afraid that fear would grip me again. If it does, He will deliver me from it as I seek Him and walk blamelessly, allowing Jesus to cover my sins with His blood.

My prayer for you is that if you need a jump start with your time with the Lord, you will find it, too.

REACHING OUT TO OUR NEIGHBORS
SEPTEMBER 2003

Do you ever feel that you can't do the evangelism thing? Do you feel it is too hard to do? Does it feel like you won't ever be able to make a difference for Jesus in someone's life?

Let me tell you a story about how God brought a neighbor to us who needs Jesus and how we began to reach out to them.

A young Muslim family moved into the duplex behind our house. They had a small daughter and the wife was pregnant. (The husband speaks pretty good English but his wife speaks very little.)

The first connection we made beyond just a "hi" in passing happened because of the tall grass in their yard. I went up to the husband and asked if he knew that he was responsible for mowing the grass. It was the beginning of the mowing season and his grass was very tall. He said he thought he was paying for his lawn to be taken care of when he paid the water and sewer bill. I explained the bill was for the water he used in his house and had nothing to do with the yard. I gave him permission to use our mower (because I knew he didn't have any) and showed him how it worked. Bob later gave him permission to use our mower any time and showed him how to get into our shed and get it whenever he needed it. Later he told us, "God bless you for being so kind to us."

When they had their new baby, Breanna and I went to their house with a gift. The husband wasn't home. We had a hard time communicating with the wife but we enjoyed our visit. She invited us in and gave us each a glazed donut and Tang to drink. We tried to talk with her as best we could without much success. She told me the baby's name three or four times and each time I repeated it back to her. I could tell by the look on her face that I just wasn't getting it! We both finally gave up!

Since then I've tried to find ways to be able to connect. I've given them produce from the garden. Once Breanna was weeding the garden and the neighbor came into the garden with the baby on her hip and the little girl beside her and began to weed with Breanna. Breanna showed her the pile to put the weeds on very perplexed as to why she was helping weed. The woman said, "No," and motioned that she wanted to take the "weeds" with her to eat. We are still wondering what kind of meal they ate that evening!

I feel it is such a privilege that God brought us this opportunity to share His love with these neighbors. I am trying to learn a few Arabic words so I can greet her the next time I see her with words in her own language. It isn't hard to share Jesus' love when God opens the doors.

You can do it, too, right in your circle of influence. Who is it that God wants you to reach out to and bless? They could be right in your own back yard!

REFLECTING THE LORD'S GLORY

OCTOBER 2003

"And we, who with unveiled faces all reflect the Lord's glory, are being transformed into his likeness with ever-increasing glory, which comes from the Lord, who is the Spirit" (2 Cor. 3:18).

This was in my devotional reading this week. The question that came to mind after I read it is, "What do I want to reflect: the world's values or the Lord's glory?" I want to reflect the Lord's glory!

The problem is that my "mirror" gets very dirty sometimes with a lot of "junk" that I focus on instead of my Savior. Some of the junk items are good things that keep me from the best thing that Jesus wants me to do. Sometimes the Lord's glory can't even shine into my heart let alone reflect out to others. Sometimes I get so caught up in the tasks at hand that I don't reflect glory because I'm too involved in what I'm doing to even notice the Lord's glory.

I want to reflect His glory. That means I have to be focused on Him to do it. We will reflect whatever is in front of our "mirror." I have to spend time with Jesus to reflect Him.

It is so easy to get sidetracked! It is so easy for me to get involved in so many "good" things and forget to draw near to God! I can't fulfill the purpose God has for me if I am not spending time with Him. I need to get His heart and receive His instructions for what He's calling me to do.

According to this verse, I have to have an "unveiled face." That means I have to take off what is there that is hampering the clear reflection. When I spend time with God in prayer and confess those things that are hindering my relationship with Him, I will be able to reflect His glory to the people I come into contact with.

The goal is to be transformed into His likeness with ever-increasing glory! The more I spend time with Jesus, the more I will become changed to be like Him. Then His glory will increase in that reflection so no one can miss it.

WELCOMING TROUBLE?
NOVEMBER 2003

In our small group, we are going through *The Purpose-Driven Life* by Rick Warren. It is an awesome book showing us the five purposes God has for our lives.

This month I want to talk to you about Day 25, "Transformed by Trouble." After reading this, I look at my troubles in a totally different way.

God uses circumstances to develop our character. He depends more on circumstances than our reading the Bible to develop character because circumstances happen all day every day. We usually read the Bible only part of the day.

It is in our darkest hours that we experience our most profound and intimate experiences of worship.

This is so true in my life. When I'm going through a deep struggle, I cling to God because He is my lifeline. It's then I realize how much I really am dependant on Him. When things are going well, it's easy to believe that I am in control of my life. Problems force me to look to God and depend on Him instead of myself.

Romans 8:28 says, "*Everything* (including trouble) *works together for good*." Rick Warren breaks this verse down so we can see what God really means by it.

We know—God is in *complete* control.

…**that God causes**—We make mistakes but God never does. He cannot make mistakes.

…**everything**—it involves ALL that happens *including our mistakes*! God can bring good out of the worst evil!

…**to work together**—not separately but together in God's plan. Some ingredients of a cake eaten separately wouldn't taste good. They would taste bitter. But if we put them together and heat it up, it becomes a delicious cake. If I give God all my distasteful, unpleasant experiences, He will blend them together and make something beautiful out of it.

...for the good—not everything in life is good but God specializes in bringing good out of it.

...to those who love God and are called—it is only for God's children, not for everyone. All things work for bad for those living in opposition to God and insist on having their own way.

...according to His purpose—What is God's purpose? To make us like His Son. Everything is permitted for that purpose. God will use whatever it takes to make us more like Christ.

Jesus went through suffering. Why do I think I should be exempt?

To be able to respond like Jesus to my circumstances is my goal. The first thing in responding like Jesus is to remember that God's plan is good. I must stay focused on God's plan and not my suffering.

I must rejoice and give thanks. I can rejoice in the Lord, not in my pain because God walks through the pain with me!

I must refuse to give up! Character-building is a slow process. I must not ask, "Why me?" but "What do you want me to learn?" Then I must trust God! I can't give up; I must grow up!

This is my prayer for all of us that we can face the difficulties focusing on Jesus and what He wants us to learn instead of wallowing in the pain.

"Jesus, help us to keep our focus on You in spite of the circumstances around us. Help us to choose to walk through the suffering, allowing You to mold us into the person You want us to be!"

AMBER IN NEPAL
DECEMBER 2003

A mber is on a four-month missionary service in Nepal until the end of this month. I had made a commitment to her to pray for her every weekday, sending her an e-mail of the prayer I was praying. Yet, about a month ago, she was really experiencing difficulty. She wrote e-mails wishing she was home and saying she was sick and could hardly get out of bed. She also said she awoke during the night with severe pain. I was pretty shook up. It was so hard for me to hear that she wasn't doing well! I wanted to fly into Nepal and take care of her.

I asked a friend to pray with me one Sunday morning. She prayed for Amber first. Then she began to pray that I would release the burden off of my shoulder and give it to God. I began weeping, not realizing up to that time how much I was carrying Amber's struggles.

The following week while I was on my way to work, a revelation came to me. I felt the Lord say to let go of Amber. I began by saying, "*Okay, Lord, I completely release Amber to You. I know I can't do anything to help her get better. I am not the one who will bring about her healing. Lord, even the prayers I pray are not what will bring her healing. Lord, It is ONLY YOU who brings about transformation. I know that You want me to pray, but I declare right now that it isn't in the prayers, but in YOU that healing comes. I release Amber and allow You to do the healing You want to do. Bring about Your purposes in Amber's life. I know You will take care of her and that she is in good hands.*"

It was a breakthrough for me. I felt much better. I didn't stop praying for Amber, but my focus changed from what I could do, to what God can and will do.

I came to this same place when Breanna was diagnosed with a brain tumor. I had to release her to Jesus and allow God to take control. I couldn't do anything about it anyway (except to pray) but still thought I could somehow do something. When I released her to Jesus, I felt that peace that comes from Him alone.

If you have a child, family member, or friend who is struggling, the place to begin is to release them to Jesus. Then you can minister to them out of what He tells you to do and not out of trying to become the "healer" and "fixer" of their situation. He is in charge. He will carry your loved one through. Trust Him! It is the best thing you can do for the one who is struggling.

Amber is doing fine now. Praise the Lord! I still send her e-mails of my prayers almost every day, but my attitude about who is in charge has changed. I gladly allow God to be who He is, because He is much better at being God than I am!

God tested Abraham with his promised son, Isaac, asking him to take Isaac and sacrifice him on the mountain. When Isaac asked where the sacrifice was, Abraham said, "*God Himself will provide the lamb for the burnt offering, my son*" (Genesis 22:8).

Abraham showed that he trusted God more than he trusted in the son God had promised him. Instead of trusting in the miracle, he trusted in the One who performed the miracle. We can do the same. God provided the way out when Abraham trusted Him completely. He will provide the way out for us, too.

God is so faithful. We can trust Him completely. Praise His Holy Name!

YOU ARE MY SUNSHINE
BREANNA'S TESTIMONY GIVEN ON DECEMBER 7, 2003

About three years ago, I woke up from a long night of entertaining my friends at my tenth birthday party sleepover. All ten of us girls stumbled upstairs for breakfast.

After breakfast, the fun night and drowsy morning made everyone spread out. I went downstairs to watch a movie with some of my friends while the others stayed upstairs.

Watching the people move across the TV, I noticed that my tongue was going numb in a tingly sort of way. I made the bad choice of trying to keep my mouth shut, fighting it, until my whole body was shaking. I looked at my friend with terrified eyes as I tried to tell her to go get my mom. She struggled to understand me, but even I couldn't comprehend what passed my lips. Finally, one girl ran upstairs to get mom. I couldn't tell who that smart girl was because my vision was going black. I passed out in a few seconds.

I woke up to find my mom telling me, "It'll be alright, Breanna, the ambulance is coming" and everyone crying their eyes out. I didn't even know what Mom was talking about.

"Why did you call the ambulance?" I asked her with horrible thoughts of my family and friends lying hurt on a cold floor. My question was never answered because the ambulance had arrived.

Suddenly, my shaky dilemma rushed back into my memory. But I knew I was alright, so I kept on telling them that I was fine and this was a big deal over nothing. But when I got to the hospital, it all changed.

My stomach somehow didn't feel like keeping down my Golden Grahams. I've never barfed so many times in one day in my life! Seven times I leaned forward and vomited the yellow and brown goop, even on the CT scan table which is so small I nearly fell off.

After awhile of testing and questions, I was allowed to go home. *Ahh*, was my first thought when I got home. I plopped onto the couch and slept the day away. I even thought it was morning when I got up. I was surprised my brothers were up at 6:30 "a.m." as I thought.

My dad's Theophostics and a music box I had received during my birthday party helped me see what Jesus had been trying to say to me. Dad probed my mind with questions and helped me hear the song Jesus was singing to me: *You are my sunshine, my only sunshine. You make me happy when skies are gray. You'll never know, dear, how much I love you. Please don't take my sunshine away.* That song was on the music box.

That song has helped me through many trials in my life. It always reminds me of His amazing love for His children.

Reflections
OF HOPE

PROCLAIMING GOD'S FAITHFULNESS

JANUARY 2004

"The LORD, the LORD, the compassionate and gracious God, slow to anger, abounding in love and faithfulness, maintaining love to thousands and forgiving wickedness, rebellion, and sin. Yet He does not leave the guilty unpunished" (Exodus 34: 6, 7).

I am so glad to serve a God who is gracious and compassionate, slow to anger, and abounding in love and faithfulness. He has shown his faithfulness to me in so many ways. I can't begin to tell you all the times when I thought things were at a hopeless state; that there was no hope for things to change or to get better, but God brought me through in such a way as to prove to me again that He will never leave me nor forsake me. Even in the pit, God is there.

I'm thankful that God doesn't *"treat (me) as (my) sins deserve or repay (me) according to (my) iniquities"* as Psalms 103:10 says. Instead He removes my sin *"as far as the east is from the west"* when I confess it to Him as Psalm 103:12 says.

I'm overwhelmed right now at the awesome God we serve! Who can compare? I am definitely not slow to anger and abounding in love. I have a hard time showing love when someone doesn't live up to my expectations. Yet God shows love and compassion to us when we fall far short of His purposes and plans for our lives. He takes those shortcomings and turns them into great strengths for His kingdom. The very things that we want to hide and not let anyone see in us are the very things God wants to use to prove that He is faithful and true.

I am committed to being open and honest in the year 2004 with those around me. I don't want to let people think more of me than I am or take credit for what God is doing in me. I want to be faithful in sharing the things God lays on my heart. I want to live more for others than for myself. I want to proclaim to the world and those around me how faithful God is. I commit to God because through Him I can do this. I will fail many times throughout the year. But God will be there to pick me up and brush me off and say, "Don't beat yourself up. Next time use My strength, not yours, and you will succeed."

Will you join me in proclaiming God's faithfulness to all generations? You are the only one who can tell the story of how God is faithful in your life. We need everyone's stories to reach all of the people God wants us to reach this next year.

AN AWESOME STORY OF GOD'S PERFECT TIMING

FEBRUARY 2004

At our women's ministry evening, we were given an opportunity to bless other women with a candle we made during the evening. I was going to take my candle to my Muslim neighbor. I talked with Bob about it. He said he felt that God wanted us to give them some money with the gift. I also prayed about what to say on the card.

We had to wait until our Christmas bonus to give the money. For some reason, this year it was late. We received it on the Monday after Christmas. Every time I looked at the card, I would ask the Lord, "What should I write on it?" I never received anything until the Tuesday after Christmas when we were getting ready to take the candle to them.

I wrote on the card, "God has blessed us this year so we want to bless you in the name of Jesus whom we serve. We are really glad to have you as neighbors. Your neighbors, Bob and Marla Brenneman and family." I put the card and the money in the envelope and set it on the kitchen counter. Bob and I went back to brush our teeth before we went to their house.

While we were getting ready, Jezra came back to our bathroom and said, "The neighbors are here." This Muslim family was at our door holding out a plate of homemade goodies for us! We were floored! The father said that he was sorry it was after Christmas. We told them that we were just getting ready to go to their house and give them our gift. We pointed to the gift on the counter.

We couldn't have planned it any better if we had worked for hours and hours on the perfect plan! They had waited because he works for so many hours in his two jobs that he has no time for visiting. We waited because of the money God told us to give them. It just "happened" that we were both giving the gift on the same night. What a great God we serve who guides our steps. The timing is in His hands!

I invited them to sit down. We visited for maybe 30-45 minutes. He told us their names again. I wrote them down this time because I have a hard time remembering them. He talked about how they struggle financially. They knew nothing of the money in the envelope on the counter. We prayed that they wouldn't be offended by the money. We trust that if God asked us to give, then He will take care of how it is received.

After I wrote the first story about this couple last summer, a lady in our church wondered if they were the Muslim couple her son, Charles, had been ministering to in our subdivision for a few years. As she described the family, I didn't think it was them.

While we were sitting there talking with the couple, Bob asked them if they knew Charles. The father said, "Char-les? He is my favorite friend; a very good friend." What a wonderful "coincidence" this was! When I told Charles' mom the next day she said, "Jesus really wants this family in the Kingdom!"

Please join me as I pray that the eyes of this family's hearts will be enlightened in order that they may know the hope to which Jesus has called them, the riches of His glorious inheritance of the saints, and His incomparably great power for them when they believe (taken from Ephesians 1:18-19).

DADDY CAN FIX IT!
FEBRUARY 2004 (CONT.)   BY BOB BRENNEMAN

In the past when doing projects around the home, I would involve my children but would really want to do it myself so I could complete the task quicker. My children would last only a short while and then want to leave. Their question was, "Dad, how much longer till we're done?" I know this is nothing unusual for children who have all kinds of things that are more entertaining than working with Dad.

My wife said that I wasn't much fun to work with. So over the years I have tried to be kinder. I have found that working alone is no fun at all. So if I wanted my children to work with me I had to change.

I have pushed myself for the last two years to get things done around the house so I could be about the Lord's business. I'm convinced now that with an attitude like that I would never get to Kingdom work. But that's another story. You can imagine that my temper has been on a short fuse.

My boys and I have been working in the basement for the past eight months. Just before Christmas we were trying to complete putting dry wall on the ceiling. Jezra and I were holding the sheets while Kyle was screwing them in place.

Three-quarter-inch copper pipes, coming from the boiler, ran parallel with, and two inches away from, the outer wall. Pointing to the spot, I told Kyle to stay close to the wall so as not to put a screw in the pipe. We positioned the next piece of dry wall. I looked at the other end to make sure that the piece was where I wanted it. Then I heard the dreaded words from Kyle, "Oh, NO!!!!!!!"

He had put the next screw through the pipe. He backed the screw out and steaming, hot water sprayed everywhere. We ran to grab a bucket.

I looked into my son's eyes in that split second and said, "It's okay, Son, I can fix it."

This happened around 11:00 a.m. I turned off the water and sent my wife to get some parts from the store while I prepared the pipes for soldering. Soldering old pipes can be tricky. The pipe must be clean and free from water. The water is the hard part.

To make a longer story short, I finished the soldering and then found out the circulator pump on the furnace wasn't working. It took two days to get it fixed. We have wood heat, so we still kept the house fairly warm, although it was pretty cold on the main floor.

After dinner I told my son again that it was okay and that I would rather have him helping me even if he makes mistakes. He was reassured and has given me permission to tell this story.

The story is not finished yet, for early the next day my Heavenly Father said in His quiet way, "*Son, I want you to help me in my Kingdom work. And Son, if you should make a mistake, Daddy can fix it.*"

MY PURPOSE STATEMENT
MARCH 2004

After reading Day 40 of *The Purpose Driven Life* by Rick Warren, one phrase stood out to me. "If God is in the center, you worship; if not, you worry. Worry is the warning light that God has been shoved to the sideline!"

I want God to be the center. One way for that to happen is to write out a purpose statement using the five purposes from the book. That is what I will attempt to do in this newsletter article.

God is the center of my life. To keep Him in the center, I will spend time daily in worship giving Him the highest place in my life. I will strive to be in His presence all day long, not just during my quiet time in the morning, by seeking His face throughout the day as things come up.

I want my character to be like Jesus. Jesus is more concerned with who I am than what I do. I will be a person who chooses to allow the fruit of the Holy Spirit to dwell in me. These fruits consist of love, joy, peace, patience, kindness, gentleness, goodness, faithfulness, and self-control. I will be quick to listen, slow to speak, and slow to get angry. When I fail, I will ask forgiveness of the Heavenly Father and of those who I may have hurt in the process.

My contribution to the body of Christ is to use my spiritual gifts to help others to walk into the freedom God has for them. I will always find ways to share with others what God has done and is doing in my life as I walk alongside them in their struggles. Other ways I will share are through my writing in the newsletter, through leading Celebrate Recovery and other groups, and possibly through writing a book in the future. Part of this contribution is to, along with my husband, raise our kids by leading them into a relationship with Jesus and helping them to connect with Him on their own. I will help them to fulfill the purpose God has for their lives by calling forth their gifts and encouraging them to walk into the place God has for them.

My communication with those outside the church will happen as God brings those divine appointments. I will deliberately reach out to friends and neighbors who don't know Jesus by becoming their friend and then showing them the Light of the World. I will continually look for ways to build relationships with others who don't know Jesus.

My community is the body of Christ at my church. I will seek to build relationships with the members here by attending or leading a small group, participating in times of fellowship, inviting people into my home, and being available to pray for the hurting.

My ultimate goal is to be more like Christ; my family is the church; my ministry is to hurting people; my mission is to bring others into the Kingdom of God; my motive is to glorify God in all I do and say.

I can only do this if I keep God at the center of my life. "For *with God nothing will be impossible!*" (Luke 1:37 NKJV). I know "*I can do ALL things through Christ who strengthens me*" (Philippians 4:13 NKJV).

FORGIVING SOMEONE FROM THE PAST

APRIL 2004

On Sunday our pastor talked about making amends and forgiving those who have hurt us. I have a story that illustrates the point that you shouldn't always go to the person and let them know they have hurt you.

Last week my family and cousins were together because my aunt had passed away. A lot of us had the same first grade teacher. By her plain clothing and head covering, she appeared to be very religious. We talked about her on Wednesday because we had all been affected by her actions.

She had very unusual discipline techniques. One of the cousins was in my class and was spanked in front of the class a few times that year. He was always getting into trouble. He would have been diagnosed with ADHD now, but back then they didn't know what to do with someone who couldn't sit still.

Another of this teacher's discipline techniques was when someone hit you, you were supposed to hit them back just as hard. My sister Jenny remembers being scolded because she wouldn't hit this other boy as hard as he had hit her!

My brother remembers when some older boys on the bus took his Popeye lunch box that had a Popeye thermos in it. They banged it around and gave it back to him. When he opened up the thermos, it was broken inside. He was too scared to tell the teacher, so he drank his chocolate milk by straining it through his teeth to keep from drinking the broken glass!

I couldn't get my thermos full of hot leftover noodles opened one morning. Too scared to ask the teacher for help, I just sat there and cried. Although after she noticed I was crying, she did come and help me open it.

Another cousin remembers saying a bad word in her class. She put soap in his mouth and wouldn't let him rinse it out for the rest of the day. He says he never said another bad word again (at least not in her class).

This teacher was moved up to 4th grade after my sister had her in first grade because she was so harsh. My sister almost had to have her twice! A few years later the teacher was fired because of her abusive ways.

At the viewing on Thursday, who should come through the receiving line but this first grade teacher! We were all dumbfounded! She looked like a kind, frail grandmother. She must be in her eighties by now. She came up to my family and shook our hands. We told her which ones of us were in her class.

Trying to understand where she may have been coming from, we asked her about her own family. She has two kids of her own. She also raised a foster son—a fourth grader of hers who had been abused in his former home and didn't know how to read. After he was taken away from his family, she and her husband raised him to adulthood.

It didn't seem like she had any clue the pain she had caused her students. It wouldn't do any good to tell her now how much she had hurt us. It would only cause her unnecessary distress. We just smiled and listened to her talk.

I have forgiven her for the hurt she caused me and my relatives. I have revealed the hurt, released the offender, and replaced the hurt with God's peace. I did all this without having to talk to the teacher at all. Seeing her last week really drove home the point that I didn't have to involve her to forgive her. I can now love her with Jesus' love. I pray she has found her peace with God, too.

Reflections
OF FAMILY

THE TUMOR HAS SHRUNK!

AUGUST 2005

Breanna's tumor has shrunk a tiny bit! This is the first time since she was diagnosed that the tumor has changed at all. God knew the exact time to bring a little bit of a miracle. Her doctor had said this kind of tumor never shrinks.

Breanna is 14 years old. This summer she began to experience a lot of fear after she realized the seriousness of what having a tumor means. When she was diagnosed, she was only 10 and never thought much about her prognosis. Her dad and I experienced all this fear 4 years ago. God had given us a peace about her tumor. We were also thankful the prognosis is that as long as the tumor doesn't grow, they won't do any treatment. After 4 years of MRI's that showed no change, our fears were put to rest for the most part.

One night last month, Breanna asked to talk with her dad and me. She said she is realizing that a tumor means death. She was scared she will miss out on so much if she dies, like getting married and having children. She wept and wept. We asked Jesus to speak to her.

She told us that one of the things He said was that her death would reach lots and lots of people. (As her parents, this was hard to hear!) Bob asked Jesus if this was true and if it brought peace. It did. Breanna kept saying, "God is using this tumor for His glory. I don't have to fear because He'll be with me. I can trust Him. He's in control." She wept for probably a half hour to 45 minutes. Afterward you could feel the peace in the room. I cried, too, feeling her fear. We prayed for healing for her tumor.

When we went for the MRI, Breanna began crying during the registration process. She felt all the fear coming back. She cried through the MRI. When we got to the doctor's office, she was more excited than anyone to hear that the tumor had shrunk. The doctor kept saying, "This just doesn't happen with this type of tumor!" She wondered if we had prayed. We said, "Yes, all the time." She told us she believes in prayer and we should keep it up.

I am amazed at the God I serve. He was so gracious in giving Breanna the victory over her fear. Just when she needed a miracle, He came through for her, showing her how much He loves her. It reminds me of the verse in Psalm 100:5, "*For the LORD is good and his love endures forever; his faithfulness continues through all generations.*" Thank you, God, that I can trust You to be real to my children as well as to me!

MY JEWEL OF THE MORNING

A POEM   AUGUST 2006

Amber Dawn
"Jewel of the morning"
My firstborn
The daughter I always wanted
The most beautiful baby in the world

Within the first 6 weeks
Severe postpartum depression
The doctor called it
Anxiety!
Sleepless nights!
My mind in a catatonic state
Four days in the hospital

This wasn't how it was supposed to be!
It wasn't how I imagined it
My fantasies about having a baby
Included waking every morning
So excited to be a mom!
Instead I began a long journey
Coming back to life
From my walk through the valley

A new beginning was emerging
Enjoying my new daughter
Instead of fighting to survive
Beginning to feel emotions again
Finding out who you were
Not just existing as your mom
But actually enjoying it

God brought me through this valley
It was a journey that I walk sometimes
But the fight isn't nearly as hard
And life isn't nearly as bad
I've found out who I am
I know whose I am
Belonging to God and finding solace in Him
As He helped me get to the root
And find healing

I didn't bond to you
Until you were about 9 months old
Then life began for us
Your excitement about exploring your world
My being able to relax and enjoy who you are

Life became more than just survival
It became an adventure
I got to know my "jewel of the morning"

We've been through a lot
In your 23 years
We've had good times
And bad times
We've been through thick and thin
And we've stayed close together
Being more than mother and daughter
We've become friends!

There are trials in your life
That you are going through
Where you feel like
Life has thrown you a curve
And you want to say,
"This isn't how it was supposed to be!
This isn't what I planned!"
And God is asking, "Will you trust me
Just as your mother does?"

God is enough
To bring you through the pain
And get to the root
So you can be free again

Don't despair
Keep trusting in Him
He'll bring you through
Because you are His
"Jewel of the morning"
Most of all!

Amber Dawn
"Jewel of the morning"
My firstborn
The daughter I always wanted
The most beautiful woman in the world

MY FIRSTBORN SON

A POEM   SEPTEMBER 2006

Kyle Ray
Long awaited
Anticipated
Firstborn son
Very late in coming
Over three weeks overdue
Thought it would never happen
When would you be born?
Would you be a boy or girl?

Finally the day came
You were a boy!
We were so excited
Worth the time we had waited

You are a deep thinker
You like to figure things out
You take your time
To make sure everything is right
You can be very stubborn and determined
To you things have to be
The way you think they should

A glimpse into the past
Three years old
We drove by a daycare center
Children were outside playing
You became very excited
Mom! Can I go there?
Kyle, those kids are dropped off
By their mothers and left there for the day
You thought a bit
Mom, you would NEVER do that,
Would you?
Your little heart couldn't imagine
Kids being away from their mothers

As your mom
I often misunderstood you
I took your quiet determination
As rebellion when sometimes
It was just who you were
I didn't always see past to
The little boy inside who
Just wanted to be loved

You were lost in the shadow
Of your younger brother
Who, because of his activity,
Was always getting into trouble
You never wanted to have
Attention focused on you
So you would hide
Trying to make the attention go away
While at the same time
Your brother was doing things
That made everyone look your way

Your sense of humor
Your outlook on life
Walking through pain and depression
And finding God to be
Your loving Heavenly Father
God is just beginning to take you
Places you could never dream
I'm watching from the sidelines
Cheering you on as you move into
The calling that God has for you

A glimpse into the future
You are standing in front of a group of people
Sharing about how much God loves them
You are telling them how God worked
In your life and brought you through
Your pain and depression
People are responding
Wanting to hear more about
Your Lord and Savior
God gets the glory
His love shines brightly
Through His son and servant
Kyle Ray
Long awaited
Anticipated
Firstborn son

MY SON JEZRA

A POEM   OCTOBER 2006

Seventeen
Sometimes a man
Sometimes still a boy

All those memories
Of when you were little
The struggles of parenting
A free-thinker
A non-conformist
A person who needed to know why

How can I forget
When you brought me joy
When I could see the blessing
God had given me in you

Three years old
I had been sick
In the hospital for a week
Too far away for you to visit
You were the most expressive
Of how glad you were
That I was home
Your prayer for years afterward
At the table before meals
"Thank you that mommy came home,"
Warmed my heart every time

Six years old
Taking the microphone
Speaking out what God put on your heart
Not afraid of the crowd listening
Boldness
Determination
My mother's heart exploding
With pride for my man of God

How can I forget
When you brought me pain
When you were defiant
Wouldn't listen to a thing
Getting you to hold still
Long enough for a nap
Was next to impossible
Curbing your need to get thrills
Out of your sisters' and brother's screams
Was hard to impress
On your energetic little heart

Nine years old
You loved to explore your world

And figure out how it worked
Always getting into things
Dangerous and daring
Never thinking of consequences
Only of the excitement
Of finding a breakthrough
And knowing an outcome

You wondered what would happen
If you lit that match
You just had to try it
Even though no one was around
Who knew the whole garage would burn
That wasn't in your plan
But since it was burning
You had to pretend
It wasn't your fault
You knew nothing about it

Looking back I wonder
Did I help you along
The path God designed
Or get in the way
Of what he was creating
In you

Sometimes I acted in anger
Only wanting you to behave
Not really seeing the treasure
That was under it all
Covered up by defiance
Overlooked by anger in me
At what you were doing
That was breaking the rule

I love who you are
And love who you are becoming
I am glad to be your mom
A privilege and honor
I do not regret a thing
Not even the tough times
It has all worked together
To bring you to the place
You are now

Seventeen
Sometimes a boy
Sometimes a man
Always my son
Always God's child

BREANNA ROSE: MY BABY

A POEM   NOVEMBER 2006

Where did the time go?
How could you be sixteen already?
Once a baby, now a mature young lady

You were a sensitive child
When your brother picked on you
And made you cry
Even in your pain you would ask,
"Do you have to punish him, Mom?"
So forgiving
So loving
So easy-going
Yet you carry burdens
Not your own
Feel other's pain
Want to take it away

Learn to carry other's burdens to Jesus
Learn to lay them at His feet
And leave them there
God places these burdens
On your heart for a reason
So you can intercede
And stand in the gap
So God can do what He wants
In your friends' lives.

On your tenth birthday
Lots of your friends
Overnight
Giggling
Screaming
Not sleeping
Morning came
Someone screamed
"Breanna is shaking and foaming at the
mouth!"
Running downstairs
As fast as I could
Not knowing what I'd find
Change had begun
Life would not be the same.

Seizure!
Ambulance!
Doctors visits!
Tests and more tests!
Tumor on your brain!
Worry upon worry
You were only ten
Would I lose you before you were grown?

The time came
When I had to release you
Into the Father's loving hands
Saying, "Not my will but Yours, Lord,
In my precious child's life.
I release her to You
Your will be done."

Six years have passed
The tumor is still there
Although it is shrinking
God has used all this
To grow you up
And make you more like Jesus
And to help us to trust God more fully.

Enjoying times together
As mother and daughter
Laughing, crying, talking
Dancing, singing
Reminiscing

Where did the time go?
It faded into the distance
We don't have yesterday
But thank you, Jesus, we have today
We will enjoy our time together
And, the Lord willing, many more years
ahead
Enjoying our relationship
Mother and daughter
Friends forever

KYLE'S DEPRESSION
MARCH 2007

All I knew was that he was very withdrawn. Months later I found out just how depressed Kyle was. He spent a lot of time in the basement watching TV, playing video games, or just sitting there doing nothing. I knew he spent a lot of time alone but he was a teenager. He was our first son. He was never very open with his feelings. I didn't think things were serious.

The next thing I know, he is asking for materials from a guest speaker, Chip Judd from ReaLife Ministries, who spoke at our church. He devoured those messages and wanted more. He asked for the CD series by Jack Frost of Shiloh Ministries that Chip Judd had referenced. He bought all of Jack Frost's CD series and listened to them. One was titled, "Experiencing the Father's Embrace." All of them talked about being set free from the wounds from childhood and being able to experience the Father God's love.

After he began listening to these messages, he spent a lot of time talking with Bob and me, wanting to know more about our experiences with the Lord. We were so surprised at the difference in him. He talked and talked about God, love, and freedom. It was such a change from the withdrawn, unhappy teen he was before. It made us realize just how bad things had been.

One day I asked him what made the change. What brought him out of his depression? He said it started when he heard Chip Judd say, "I don't have bad days anymore." Kyle said, "When I heard that, I thought, I want that! I don't want to feel down anymore." He began to listen to all Chip had to say because he wanted to stop the bad days. It drove him to Father God's love. He experienced God's transforming power and hasn't been the same since.

This experience has again solidified my trust in God to take care of my children. He is big enough to deal with any issues they struggle with. He loves them more than we do. I can relax, knowing that they are in His hands.

In 3 John 1:4 it says, "*I have no greater joy than to hear that my children are walking in the truth.*" There is also no greater joy than to see your children experience God for themselves. Thank you, God, for your love for our children. Help us to continue to put them in Your hands and trust You to do great things in their lives.

STEWARDING EMOTIONS

FEBRUARY 2008   BY BOB BRENNEMAN

The other day I was making mistakes listening to measurements for sheeting a roof. My first response for years has been to blame the one on the roof for my mistakes. I too often waste such trials instead of growing through them. However the Spirit is patiently working on a response in me that would bring honor to the Father. Emotions of anger and self preservation surface first, far too easily. I am gently reminded each time that this is not the proper spiritual response. The Holy Spirit has revealed that a proper response must come from my spirit, not the soul or the natural man. The soul (being the mind, will, and emotions) cannot perceive the spiritual for they are spiritually discerned (1 Cor. 2:14,15). But, as verse fifteen says, we have the mind of Christ.

This time I was walking in the Spirit because I stayed calm. I was able to see what the Spirit was seeing. I confessed the error of not hearing correctly. Then I said, "Lord, how many times have I heard You incorrectly when you were communicating to me?"

Later that day I was reminded of a chance for new employment a year or so ago.

It had looked appealing because I was having sporadic employment. I had asked the Lord if I should take it, but the answer was no. I recently discovered that job position was laid off. The Holy Spirit whispered to me and said, "See, you sometimes hear very well!" I was overcome with His fatherly tenderness. That simple statement chased away self-pity that day.

The next day I was a part of a church meeting. Our pastor opened with prayer. He then asked if we had a need that he could pray for. I couldn't think of any for myself but before the meeting was over, I should have. The pastor stated that any time spent focusing on the Lord always sets up the meeting to be more productive. I instead, during the evening, opened my mouth and steered the conversation down a rabbit trail. I was frustrated with my inability to communicate, so I tried again with no better results. I finally said, "I'm going to keep my mouth shut." I left feeling frustrated and defeated.

That night sleep kept eluding me. I could feel self-pity wrap its arms around me. I was able to sleep some before I had to go to work. In the morning my self-inflicted wound was oozing words of self-hatred. The bottle filled with the self-pity I had been collecting turned into a weight on my shoulders that sucked away any joy still remaining. I knew that I should not yield to this evil. All day darkness increased.

As I was driving home from work, I remembered something someone had said at the meeting, " When we say no to the Spirit, we are managing the Spirit but when we say yes to the Spirit, the Spirit is managing us." I lifted my eyes to the sky and said YES to the Spirit.

The Spirit's response to me was, "Bob, you need to do what you said at the meeting, 'Keep your eyes focused on the Lord.'" I asked the Spirit how I lost my focus. The Spirit responded, "You were beginning to care more about what people thought of you than what I think of you." I quickly repented and the weight on my shoulders lifted.

Sunday a prophetic friend gave me a word from the Lord that I needed to use the authority of the Lord. Praise God for a quick turnaround.

JOURNEY OF A TEENAGER

JANUARY 2009   BY BREANNA BRENNEMAN

I was ten years old when we found out about my brain tumor. I was too young to understand what a tumor could mean. If I did, I think I hid it behind a mask of jokes, telling myself it wasn't a big deal. All the things I did to protect myself from the reality of it came crashing down at age fourteen. I am an Overachiever. I always use perfection as my standard. In eighth grade, I began comparing myself to that standard of perfection and found I came up short. I quickly spiraled into a depression. I thought no one would love me if I wasn't perfect in everything. I knew in my mind that God loved me, but that truth had not penetrated my heart. I remember sobbing one night because I felt so unloved. I was crying out for someone to love me for who I was and not expect so much of me. I was getting nowhere. I kept returning to the same thing: I'm not perfect and therefore not loved.

I spent months like that at school. I became very good at plastering a smile on my face. It was easy to hide my feelings at school. There were so many distractions and I had work to do. My emotions couldn't get in the way. I couldn't ask for help from anyone, because that would prove to them that I was imperfect. I didn't feel like I could talk to anyone. I felt guilty about wanting to share my heart because I didn't want to burden anyone. The only place I wasn't happy all the time was home. There were no distractions at home. All my problems stared me right in the face. I was very quiet around the house. When I look back on it now, I remember seeing my mother's concerned face or my father's sad gaze. I couldn't see the love in their faces. I made myself blind to it. When school got out for the summer, I began writing in my journal. I began by reading a Bible verse and then writing down what I thought about it. The first verse I read was 1 Kings 8:27: *"Can it be that God will actually move into our neighborhood? Why, the cosmos itself isn't large enough to give you breathing room, let alone this Temple I've built"* (MSG).

Here's part of my response:

He wants to dwell in me...ME!!! I find myself to be so worthless. I mean I know that I have value but I feel like if I'm not perfect... He won't love me. But He does! His love is higher than the tallest mountain, deeper than the Marianas Trench! There is NO comparison!

This is when my situation began to turn around. I began to realize what my tumor could mean. "The fear struck me not too long ago. I realized what it means...Death," I wrote in my journal. I began seriously wanting to talk to my parents. This fear haunted me during the day and tormented me at night. I couldn't escape from it. I reasoned that everyone dies, so how could I expect to be spared?

Finally, I opened up to my parents. It began with telling my mom I wanted to talk and then me bursting into tears. During our talk, we prayed, and I heard God promise me that He would take my tumor away. I did not understand it at the time. I thought God meant He would prepare me for my death. I was still resigned to the fact that the tumor would kill me. But I knew in that moment that He would be faithful and fulfill His promise to me. I didn't know how or when, but I knew. After that night my faith was renewed. I felt solidly grounded in His love for me. I finally realized that perfection is not what He wants. He wants my heart. He wants me! I was able to be myself and I was happy. However, behind my happiness, there was a fear of the upcoming doctor's appointment at the children's hospital.

The week before the appointment my fear continued to build. The thought of the tumor growing was always in the back of my mind. I kept thinking I had symptoms of the tumor growing, like increased headaches and my left eye drooping more. I was scared. The Sunday before the appointment I played my violin at the church and the speaker prayed for me. He prayed that the people around me would be supportive on my next doctor visit. The prayer touched me and my fear subsided for a moment. But, his prayer was forgotten the night before the appointment.

I wrote in my journal at 11:00 pm that I was scared. I was praying for peace, but my worry was still there. I was so afraid of what Dr. Smith would say. I read Psalms 90:15: "*Make us glad for as many days as you have afflicted us, for as many years as we have seen trouble.*" But it didn't help. The fear still loomed over me, making my spirit troubled and restless. I remember watching the hours tick by. I had to get up at 5 o' clock to be there on time. I watched 1 a.m. pass, then 2, and 3. Finally at 3:30, I fell asleep, only to be awakened an hour and half later. I tried to sleep in the car, but I couldn't. The fear clung to me like a rotting odor. I couldn't get my mind to rest enough so that I could sleep. When we arrived at the hospital, I broke down and cried. I cried like a child afraid of the boogeyman. We had to go to the MRI before we met with Dr. Smith. I cried through the MRI. The only consolation I had was the worship music they let me listen to. God made each song help calm me down.

After the MRI, we had to wait an hour for the prints from the scan. We went out into the courtyard. I still had tears running down my face. My dad comforted me with the prophesy God gave him years ago when we found out about the tumor, "*The little boy inside her will be a great warrior for the Lord.*" Our interpretation was that my son will be a great warrior for God. That means that I would have to be old enough to get married, which means that the tumor would not kill me now, if ever. My tears subsided and the fear was not as apparent. I had a foundation to stand on, reassurance from God that I would live. I went to the appointment with a peace that only God could give. Dr. Smith came into the exam room with a baffled expression on her face. She showed us the scans of my brain and how the tumor had shrunk. It was just a couple millimeters but it shrunk none the less!

Today, I would not trade having a brain tumor with anyone. Having this tumor has caused me to mature and come closer to God. I thank God for it and I hope He will use me to help others who struggle with illnesses. What God taught me through this is that even in hard times, God loves me and He will never stop. We can't do anything to make Him love us more or less. He will love us eternally.

DEATH OR LIFE: WHICH WILL WE CHOOSE?

FEBRUARY 2009

Our associate pastor asked us to have a family discussion in front of everyone around a table set up like a brunch with muffins and orange juice. We were given three questions to discuss. Why do we believe that Mary was a virgin? Why is it an important part of our theology? Why might God have chosen to do things this way concerning His Son's birth?

We were given 5 minutes to discuss each question. Bob, Breanna, and I, along with three of our friends were part of the brunch discussion. I began by thanking our friends for joining us for our brunch, saying I had been thinking about Mary. It was quite easy to talk to the people around the table and forget that there were others present.

The last question stuck with me, so I focused my comments on that one. I began to think about why God brought His Son into the world through a woman. I thought all the way back to Eve and the first woman God created. Sin came through Eve. She believed the serpent's lie and took the forbidden fruit. She was deceived along with her husband. Because of sin, the human race needed redemption. God's plan for redemption happened even before sin came. He always has a plan for redemption in every situation.

Think about the curse God placed on women. God said, *"I will greatly increase your pains in childbearing; with pain you will give birth to children"* (Genesis 3:16).

Sin came to the world through a woman. Her curse was pain in childbirth. God chose to use this curse to bring His Son into the world. Redemption of the world came through a woman through childbirth, the very thing God had cursed.

Mary gave life to the Savior of the world. Eve brought death through sin. Death. Life. Each brought through a woman. Each woman made a choice that affected all humankind. God had it planned from the beginning. There is no situation so hopeless that cannot be redeemed.

To the serpent He said, "*I will put enmity between you and the woman, and between your offspring and hers; he will crush your head, and you will strike his heel*" (Genesis 3:15).

Eve believed a lie and was deceived. Mary chose to believe the Truth. Because of this, God brought redemption through Mary's son, the Son of God.

Adam, the first man, followed Eve into sin. He believed the lie along with her. He didn't stand up for what was right and true. He didn't protect his wife from the enemy. The Bible tells us in Romans that it was Adam's responsibility. "*Therefore, just as sin entered the world through one man, and death through sin, and in this way death came to all men, because all sinned... How much more did God's grace and the gift that came by the grace of the one man, Jesus Christ, overflow to the many*" (Romans 5:12,15).

Joseph, Mary's husband, stood by Mary even when it was hard to believe the story she told him. He also believed the Truth the angel told. He was there for Mary while she was pregnant. He went through the hardship they must have faced having a baby out of wedlock. He protected them both by fleeing to Egypt to get away from Herod. He helped nurture and raise the Son of God with Mary. Instead of bringing death, Mary and Joseph brought life. They parented the Redeemer of the world. Through this Redeemer, the whole world has the opportunity of eternal life.

Every day we all have the opportunity to choose life or death. Every circumstance we face has choices that lead to life or death. Some are more obvious than others. Sometimes it can take us years to see the impact. Choose life. Choose hope. Choose faith. Choose redemption. God did.

The results are amazing.

I'm so glad God is such a redeeming God. He takes our messes and our sins and turns them into victory and redemption. I have seen this happen in my life when I surrendered to Him. The very things that brought me death have been used to bring life to others.

Thank you, God, for bringing redemption through fallible humans. You could have left Adam and Eve in their misery and therefore left the human race in misery but you didn't. You had a plan from the very beginning. Thank you for taking us from death to **LIFE** in **YOU**!

CONTENTS IN DETAIL

Printed in the United States
149769LV00001B/5/P